Carving Realistic Animals
with Power

Frank C. Russell

77 Lower Valley Road, Atglen, PA 19310

Dedication

To my father, Clarence M. Russell, whose understanding, knowledge, and love for animals was expanded then passed to his progeny. To him, my love and thanks.

To all animals, both domestic and wild, who for so long have been companions, soul mates, providers, and sources of enjoyment. To the extinct species who can no longer give joy and benefaction to this world. To all, my love and apologies.

Copyright © 1994 by Frank C. Russell.
Library of Congress Catalog Number: 94-66201

Printed in Hong Kong.
ISBN: 0-88740-637-8

Published by Schiffer Publishing, Ltd.
77 Lower Valley Road
Atglen, PA 19310
Please write for a free catalog.
This book may be purchased from the publisher.
Please include $2.95 postage.
Try your bookstore first.

We are interested in hearing from authors
with book ideas on related subjects.

CONTENTS

INTRODUCTION

I wrote this book on carving animals for several reasons: first and foremost, I love animals, second, I am a power carver, third, I am continuously asked about the power techniques and methods that I use, and fourth and finally, I can't get teaching out of my system.

Although I still hunt deer and turkeys for the enjoyment of the hunt and because I like venison and wild turkey to eat, more often than not, I "hunt" with nothing but a camera. I find more peace, contentment, and creative urge when alone in the woods or the swamps than in any other place. Foolish though it may sound, a greater understanding of myself has come from a better understanding of nature and things natural.

It excites me to know that I can study the animals, their actions, their habitats, and take what lore I need from them for my art. It is equally exciting to know there is so much more to go back for ... that I can always go back to the well and drink again, so to speak. *Unless, of course, a new housing development or mall suddenly appears while I'm away!*

I would like to give special thanks to the Foredom Electric Company of 16 Stony Hill Road in Bethel, Connecticut for their kind indulgence and cooperation. Unless otherwise noted, all products displayed and used throughout this book are available through this company and/or one of their many dealerships throughout this country and the world.

I SAFETY

Create a safety conscious atmosphere for yourself in the shop area. Look around the shop or area where you work. Is there a place for everything and is everything in its place?

Fire

One of the biggest considerations for the shop area is a fire hazard. If you allow wood dust resulting from power sanding or the carving process to collect and cover everything, a fire can result from an electrical spark, a lighting fixture, the flame or element of a heating unit, or even to the uninvited pipe or cigarette smoking of an unheeding visitor.

Accessory Placement

If you have as many visitors to your workplace, shop, or studio as I do, you have a legitimate concern for their safety. Consider anything that can be touched or stumbled over by a visitor, you may be surprised at dangers that you live with daily, and take for granted because of your familiarity with them.

Panic Buttons

If you have students or share a studio with other people, install one or more emergency shut-down switches, usually with red covers around the shop and make sure everyone knows their locations. Then, if someone gets into trouble with a machine, from a table saw to a flexible shaft carving machine, power can be interrupted quickly at a point away from the problem. This eliminates the need to run across the room or work area to where the problem exists before cutting power.

First Aid

Maintain a well stocked first aid kit, and be sure everyone connected with the workplace know its location, its contents, and how to use the contents, before any accident occurs.

If you don't have a smoke detector, install one. If you already have one, test it periodically to make sure it functions, especially if it's a battery operated device.

Eyes

It goes without saying that when you generate dust and wood particles over which you have no control, you should have a protective barrier between you and the point of generation. Since you don't have absolute control over the wood particles being thrown from a given carving bit, you never know exactly where any given particle of wood dust or sliver of wood is going to go. So, as a precaution, shield your eyes with a good pair of safety glasses or goggles. I find goggles or a face shield too cumbersome and uncomfortable. I prefer safety glasses with side shields. I also prefer glass lenses as opposed to plastic lenses for two reasons. First, I always end up scratching the plastic lenses, and find the scratches distracting while I work. Second, most of the plastic protective eyewear I have used has a tendency to have a static attraction for the fine dust that I generate and have to be cleaned more often than do the glass lensed protective eyewear.

Lungs

I had to be frightened, breathless, and hospitalized before I had sense enough to deal with proper dust collection and disposal in my studio. As crude as it is to speak of, I could in no way exert myself before I began coughing up great globules of greenish sputum. As simple an occurrence as laughter would cause me to have coughing spells that would rival any hard-core cigarette smoker. For weeks I refused to believe that the coughing had anything to do with my lungs, other than perhaps a "lingering" cold. Chest X ray negatives revealed two dark spots in my lungs that were described as possible cancer. I soon found myself lying in a hospital bed with a total stranger holding a syringe the size of a jack hammer, telling me how he was going to drive it in my chest to get a lung sample for a biopsy. He was told in no uncertain terms that he was indeed **not** going to drive that thing in any part of my body, and if he came closer, I would call the police.

Somewhere during the discussion, he conceded, asked me to get out from under the bed, and promised he would first try a medicinal application that might cause sputum and anything else foreign to be expelled from the lungs, if indeed there was anything foreign. They kept a close watch on me and my "exhalations", and long story made short, the next X ray session revealed an absence of dark spots on my lungs.

Analysis revealed the dark spots to be globules of wood dust formed from the large quantities of dust I inhaled during carving and sanding operations that I performed daily without any protection and gave absolutely no thought to.

Apparently, the lungs work on foreign objects in much the same way that an oyster deals with a speck of sand, coating and recoating the sand until it creates a pearl. My lungs had gathered the dust particles together to form masses that showed as dark spots on an X ray, giving the first impression that my lungs were cancerous.

I have an annual X ray now, and I'm happy to say that my lungs have remained perfectly clear since those dark spots occurred in the late 1970s. However, I was told then that older, weaker, and less healthy lungs might have led to a different outcome.

Give serious thought and consideration to the results of ignoring dust accumulation, collection, and/or disposal problems before you locate, and begin to operate, your work station.

Clothing & Hair

Loose clothing is essential to comfort in most cases, but clothing too loose can be a detriment to carving if you catch an unbuttoned shirt front in a rotating carving machine. Depending on the position(s) you carve in, be aware of such things as loose or unbuttoned sleeves, jewelry, neckpieces, ties, and above all, long hair.

I saw the unfortunate result of a young man whose hair got caught in the spindle of a high speed drill press — before he could react in any way, a very large chunk of hair and scalp was ripped from his head. I'm sure no further description is necessary. If you have long hair, and work with or around any rotating device, tie your hair back or wear a head net.

Vigilance

I was once guest speaker for a business men's meeting. Along with the speech, I was asked if I would demonstrate some of the rotary power carvers and techniques that I used to gain my livelihood.

Attired in my best bib and tucker, I delivered an awe inspiring speech, then plunged right into the demonstrative portion of my presentation. An older gentleman asked for a closer look, so I bent over to afford him a better view ... it's difficult to present yourself as a professional while a handpiece with a carbide cutter winds up your tie, then beats out the "Battle Hymn of the Republic" on your Adam's apple.

The actual incidences where lack of vigilance or attention has resulted in a cut, bruise, torn clothing, or broken machinery have been relatively few, but their occurrences have been frequent enough to serve as reminders of worse things that might have happened or could happen.

II TOOLS & ACCESSORIES

Power Tools

Flexible Shaft Machine — a general purpose machine. Before the advent of the higher RPM micro motor machines, the flexible shaft machine did everything from hogging out, to finish shaping, sanding, and texturing. By way of description, the machine used throughout this book has a 1/8 horsepower ball bearing motor capable of variable speeds up to 18,000 RPM controlled with a solid state foot control or a table top manual control.

Micro Motor Machines — are best used for lighter, more precise and more detailed work. The motor is housed in the handpiece. This gives the unit a much greater area of mobility, flexibility, and dexterity than does the anchored handpiece of the flexible shaft machine. However, the unit does not have anywhere near the power of a flexible shaft machine, and costs two to three times as much, depending on where it is purchased.

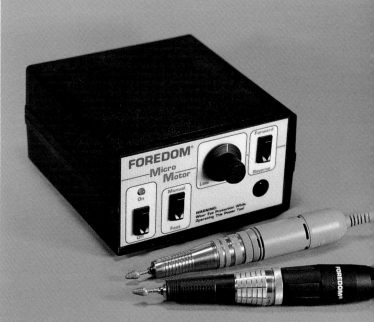

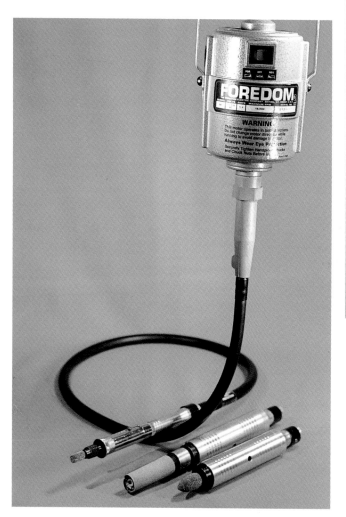

The handpieces shown with the control unit are rated for 45,000 RPM and 35,000 RPM and have 1/8" and 3/32" collet sizes.

The 45,000 RPM handpiece is preferred by the author, because I maintain that the higher the RPM, the smoother the cut, which is most desirable when texturing hair, fur, or feathers. Higher RPM also gives me a quicker, cleaner cut when I am finish shaping. With my preference for the precision of high RPM work, I rarely, if ever, use a foot control and reduce speed only when using a sanding drum, cleaning a bit, or shaping a stone bit.

Complete setups including a control unit, handpiece, a foot control, two collets, an extra set of motor brushes, an accessory/handpiece tray, and safety glasses are available from the manufacturer.

The handpieces shown are those preferred and used by the author. The larger 1" diameter, 5.5" long, seven ounce handpiece is used for heavy duty operations such as roughing out and large area sanding applications. However with an additional set of 8 collets (collar-like inserts that act as a clamping chuck to hold a bit shank) that range in sizes from 1/16" through 1/4", every aspect of power carving can be accomplished.

The smaller 3/4" diameter, 6" long, four ounce handpiece is ideal for medium to light duty application and for texturing. Four collet sizes from 1/16" through 1/8" are available, along with a 3 mm size.

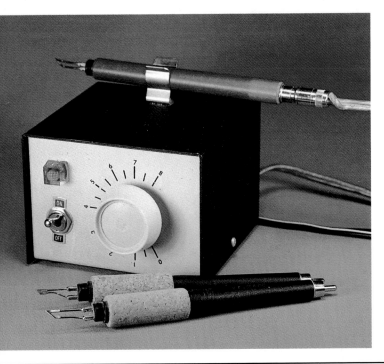

Woodburner

Choose a woodburner with a variable heat control that is separate from the power switch. When I shut the woodburner off in the middle of a burning session, I want to be able to go back to the same heat setting that I was using without having to remember where I set it in the first place. *The unit shown was built for the author by an electrical engineering friend who designed it with an extra heavy duty transformer in the control unit.*

There are many units available on the market, and the better ones will satisfy all the following criteria. The unit of choice should have:

a variety of woodburing tips available,

a heavy duty transformer,

a heat control separate from the power switch,

a small handpiece that allows comfort and flexibility, and a handpiece with a handle that doesn't heat up with prolonged use.

It's difficult to burn any detail with repeated accuracy when you're moving your hand further and further up the handle to get away from the heat that's working its way up the handle towards you.

POWER CARVING ACCESSORIES

Carving Bits

I offer the following descriptions of bits merely by way of introduction to the beginner, and suggest you experiment whenever possible with various bits, to ascertain their capabilities as well as your own. Note what it takes to achieve a particular cut or result with each bit, and the effort and type of stroke it requires. You will find this preliminary practice adds greatly to your power carving knowledge and to the results you desire.

I'm always in search of the perfect bit. I love to pick up a new type or a shape that catches my eye and put it through its paces. To date, however, I have always returned to the same tried and true sizes,

shapes, and grits that have produced so well and consistantly for me in the past. The more I carve, the less I feel the need to own every bit ever produced. The bit categories and shapes that follow are those most used for my carvings.

Rough Shaping	Finish Shaping & Smoothing	Texturing
Tungsten Carbide Burr	Ruby Carvers	Stones
Stump Cutters	Diamond Carvers	Ruby Carvers
	Stump Cutters	Diamond Carvers
		Stump Cutters

Tungsten Carbide Burr

These bits are available in a variety of shapes and shape sizes, and may be obtained in coarse and fine grits. The bit shank (shaft) is obtainable in 1/8" or 1/4" diameter. The shapes I use most and recommend for a beginner are the flame, taper, and cylinder shapes.

For rough shaping and wasting away stock, these bits are among the few that can be safely hand-held and still give the carver fast, controlled stock removal. *Caution! These bits can remove wood, flesh,*

or particles of clothing with almost equal ease, so don't force or cut beyond the capability of the bit. You are not a chain saw!

The manufacturer suggests cleaning these bits with a torch, burning away residue, and then brushing the bits with a stiff brush after they have cooled. Another method is to spray them thoroughly with oven cleaner, let them set, and then brush with a stiff bristle or fine wire brush.

Ruby Carvers

Ruby mineral abrasives are sorted, then bonded to a metal core shape, usually with a 3/32" shaft. These are the bits of choice for detail and finish carving on all of the animals that I carve.

Diamond Carvers

These bits are constructed in the same manner as the ruby carvers, but use industrial diamond particles as an abrasive. As a rule, diamond carvers are more expensive than ruby carvers, but seem to last longer and come in a greater variety of smaller shapes.

Diamond carvers are available in different shaft diameters, so be sure you have a handpiece collet for the size you buy. Usually, suppliers (whether dental or woodcarving) will identify the size and type. If not, ask before you buy. FG means Friction Grip and is a 1/16" diameter shaft commonly used by dentists. HP indicates Hand Piece or colletted grip and is a 3/32" diameter shaft.

Diamond carvers are the bits of choice for deepening detail in areas such as ear cavities, nostrils, mouths, and areas of overlaying fur. The inverted cone shapes often work well for fur or hair texturing.

Some recommended shapes to begin with are smaller flame-shapes, inverted cones, and balls.

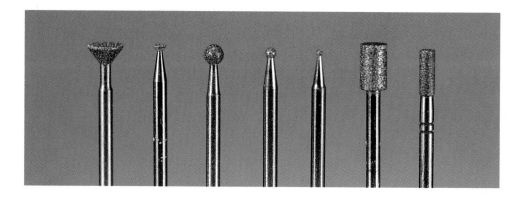

Stone Bits

These bits are made of a shaped mineral composition (commonly aluminum oxide) mounted on steel shafts. The grit is finer and gives a very smooth finish. Shaft size is 3/32" diameter for most small to medium stone bits, with 1/8" diameter shafts for most of the larger stone bits. *Stone bits vary greatly in texture of grit and quality of construction.*

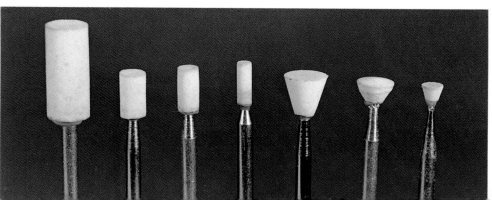

Stump Cutters

These bits are made of steel, and have serrated cutting edges that remove and allow shaping and stock smoothing remarkably well. The cylindrical shapes lend themselves very well to texturing hair and fur, making deep "v" bottomed cuts, and ledge cuts. The flame and pear shapes do well for finish shaping.

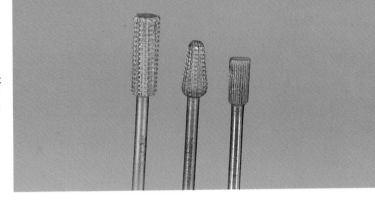

Defuzzing Pads and Cleaning Brushes

Depending on the type of wood used, these bits and/or bit mandrels (bit mandrels are shafts that hold the defuzzing pads) may not be necessary, but they are a must for anyone who carves with basswood, for example. The fiberous grains of basswood stand away from the detailing or texturing surface and must be cleaned away or made to lay back down. This can be accomplished either with a rotary defuzzing pad or a bristle brush that is run in the opposite direction of the cut, with the grain, and away from the end of the grain where ever possible.

Again, depending on the type of wood being carved, and/or while using certain bit types, these defuzzing pads and bristle brushes are a must. Defuzzing or brush cleaning should be done at a medium to slow speed so as not to remove fine details or carved surfaces.

BIT SHAPES

Once the carver learns to use a particular shape for a resultant cut, it becomes as automatic as the selection of a "V" gouge for a sharp bottomed cut, a "U" gouge for a round bottom cut, or a knife just to waste away unwanted stock. If I could only have two bit shapes, I would choose the flame-shaped first and the ball-shaped next. Depending on the angle of the handpiece, the desired cut with a flame-shaped carver can be V-shaped or U-shaped. Any area of an animal can be finish shaped and finish detailed with a flame-shaped carver.

Practice with the flame bit, and learn how versatile a tool it is. Select a speed that feels comfortable, try different carving strokes at that speed, and note the result. Next, experiment with different speeds, strokes, and handpiece angles. Note the result of the cuts, and what was needed to maintain the control it took to get a particular result. Practice with a variety of bit shapes, and soon, proper selection to your way of carving becomes automatic.

The small ball bit is as versatile a bit as is the flame-shaped. It is best used for relieving and shaping the deep hollows such as nostril cavities, ear depressions/indentations, and pupil depressions. If the eyes have detailed pupils just a slight touch is sufficient to relieve each pupil indentation. Again, practice with this bit until you are familiar with its use to your way of carving.

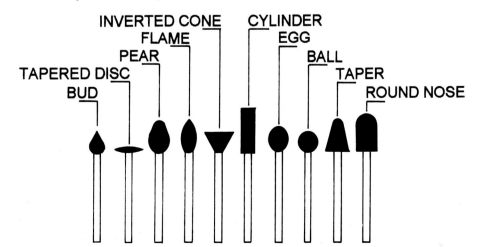

BIT SIZE

The size of the bit selected is determined by the scale of the area being carved — selection of an undersized ball bit for example will be just as inconvenient as the selection of a "U" gouge that is too small or too shallow. Try to match the bit diameter to the size desired for the bottom of an area to be cut.

BIT GRIT

Grit of the bit will determine the smoothness of finish that the surface of the carved area will receive. Selection of proper grit will save both time and effort — if the area to be carved is a rough-out or rough shape operation, there is no need for rough shaping with a fine grit bit when the area will undergo several more shaping operations with finer detail bits.

Power Tool Accessories

This section may be called accessories, but in reality, they are necessities.

Machine Hanger — every flexible shaft machine has to be hung or anchored at the motor end, or control will be ungainly and the torque of the turning motor will cause it to roll around.

Handpiece Rest or Hanger — a handpiece needs to go into a holding device to keep it out of the way, to give it a place to wind down without having to hold it while waiting for it to stop, and as a time saver in that the carver goes to the same convenient spot each time to retrieve it. When I'm carving, I don't like to have to wait for a machine to stop before I can lay the handpiece down.

Handpiece Cradles — keeps the extra unattached handpieces from rolling around, getting in the way, and/or rolling off the work surface onto the floor. When I begin to carve I set up several flexible shaft handpieces (large and small) so that I can gain quick and easy access to them as I carve.

Accessory Tray — keeping all the small accessories, such as lock pins, dressing stones, and bit cleaners localized, saves time and energy from sorting through the pileups of "treasure" that I accumulate on my work surface as I carve a piece.

Bit Stand — necessary to hold an assortment of bits within easy reach for exchange as needed in the handpiece.

Abrasive Cleaner — a block of rubber used to clean sanding devices, ruby carvers, and stone bits. Always use a slow speed, or the rubber builds up and literally wraps the bit head and shank up in rubber.

Wet stick — a mineral block that when soaked in water is quite effective for cleaning diamond and ruby carvers. Adjust the speed for maximum effect, usually a slower speed is most effective.

Dust Mask, Exhaust Fan and/or Dust Collector — it goes without saying that a dust collection or dust protection device is the most important investment for your health. Within a very short period of time the entire studio will be blanketed with a layer of fine dust particles if not properly controlled or exhausted. I don't smoke, but every year that I go for a physical, my family doctor's first concern is for my lungs. He knows what I do for a living.

Dressing Stone (Silicon Carbide) — this is a pre-shaped carborundum block with various sized grooves on its surfaces to hold a stone bit in place while it is being shaped. Use a medium speed when reshaping and always clean a reshaped stone with the rubber abrasive cleaning block.

Shadow Lamp — a source of bright light that can be aimed across the work directly opposite to your carving hand, giving deep shadow to any indentation or texture operation. A lamp such as this will save much movement and shifting of the piece under regular studio light that casts direct light and little shadow as you try to check the progress of your texturing work.

Speed Control Units — essential to some sanding and finishing operations. Foot control allows a greater amount of freedom in that the only movement required is by the foot. The hand or table top controller requires that one hand be freed to regulate speed before resuming work, requiring a break in concentration and time. The manner in which one carves, and the carver's physical preference, dictates which control unit is the more desireable.

Among the things many carvers have in common is that they like to build and tinker as well as carve. This is reflected in the many questions I receive at seminars and shows about the accessories I have built.

So, to these intrepid souls I present and dedicate this section on building "homebrew" accessories. I include a few of the more convenient ones for those who would rather build than buy.

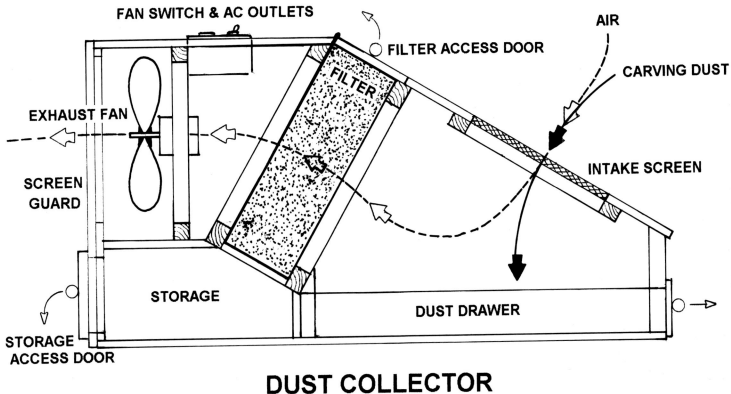

FAN SWITCH & AC OUTLETS

FILTER ACCESS DOOR

AIR

CARVING DUST

FILTER

EXHAUST FAN

INTAKE SCREEN

SCREEN GUARD

STORAGE

DUST DRAWER

STORAGE ACCESS DOOR

DUST COLLECTOR
(SCHEMATIC)

Dust Collector Construction Notes

The overall size of the box will depend on the size of the filter chosen, and whether or not you choose to include a dust drawer and storage area under the fan(s). The box illustrated is 16" high, 24" wide, and 32" long. The storage area is used to house power cords and some power carving accessories that are used during shows, demonstrations, and seminars.

A 4" x 12" x 24" filter was used only because I was given a good price on a case lot of that particular size. *Any heating and ventilating supply firm should be able to supply the filter or filter source to fit your need.*

A sixty-degree slant was given to the filter to allow dust gathered and held against the intake side of the filter to more easily fall back into the dust tray. If I notice dust beginning to build against the filter and I'm not able to take the filter out at that time, a few sharp slaps against the sides of the box usually cause most of the dust to fall back into the dust tray.

Two bathroom ventilation fans were used for air movement, but smaller "squirrel cage" type fans work just as well. *Two major considerations here are the amount of air moved and noise — get as quiet and forceful a fan as you can find. Size and weight are additional considerations if you have to move the unit from show to show, seminar to seminar, or demonstration to demonstration as I do.*

No material of any critical consequence was used. All wooden materials used were leftover or scrap pieces found in the shop. The plywood was 3/8", good on one side for all sides of the box. Where necessary, all framing supports and braces were 3/4" pine. Where thickness of stock allowed, 1" and 1 1/4" sheetrock screws and aliphetic resin glue were used. In exposed surface areas the screw heads were countersunk, filled with wood putty, and sanded to match the surface. In areas where thickness of stock would not allow screws, glue and small finish nails were used.

Both intake and exhaust screen guards were made from 1/4" hardware cloth (wire mesh).

A double outlet box was used to house a switch for the fan, and three outlets to accommodate the light and carving accessories that were attached later. *The exact location of the switch/outlet box is up to each builder. I put it on the top of the unit because I knew I would be transporting it with all the other accumulated junk that I have to carry to and from shows, demos, and seminars, and felt the switch would enjoy a greater longevity on the top. I have made others that were permanent fixtures in my studios, and installed the switch/outlets on the side, which allows me to arrange (pile ?) more accessories on the top.*

Twelve gauge copper wire was used throughout, including the power cord. All electrical connections were grounded back through the power cord to the plug. *This is not the place to skimp, or make erroneous connections! If you don't know how to safely wire according to code, get someone to either do it for you, or to advise and inspect after you have wired it.*

Dust Collector Parts List *

1 heavy duty filter *The size of the filter determines the size of the collector housing*
1 or 2 exhaust fans with mounting brackets
1 SPST 120v switch with outlet
1 duplex outlet
1 double metal outlet box with cover punched for 2 duplex   outlets
1 heavy-duty power cord
12-gauge copper hookup wire as needed
3 feet of 24" wide hardware cloth for intake and exhaust screens
3 1/2" PVC pipe clips to hold arm rest frame
1 length of 1/2" PVC pipe as wide as collector box for arm rest frame
2 1/2" PVC pipe caps for arm rest frame
1 strip of foam rubber pipe insulation for 1/2" pipe for arm rest

1" sheetrock screws, as needed
1.1/4" sheetrock screws, as needed
1.1/8" finish nails or brads, as needed
3 small drawer pulls for dust drawer, and storage and filter doors
2 spring loaded hinges for storage enclosure door
3 small 3" hinges for filter access door
3/8" AC plywood for collector housing, enclosure walls, and/or fan frame
3/4" Spruce or Pine stock for frames, braces, and dust drawer sides and ends.

All parts suggested above were parts used for the dust collector described here, and may be changed to suit the builder as need dictates, as may the construction outline itself. Any alternative part, size, or construction method that better suits the builder's needs should be used.

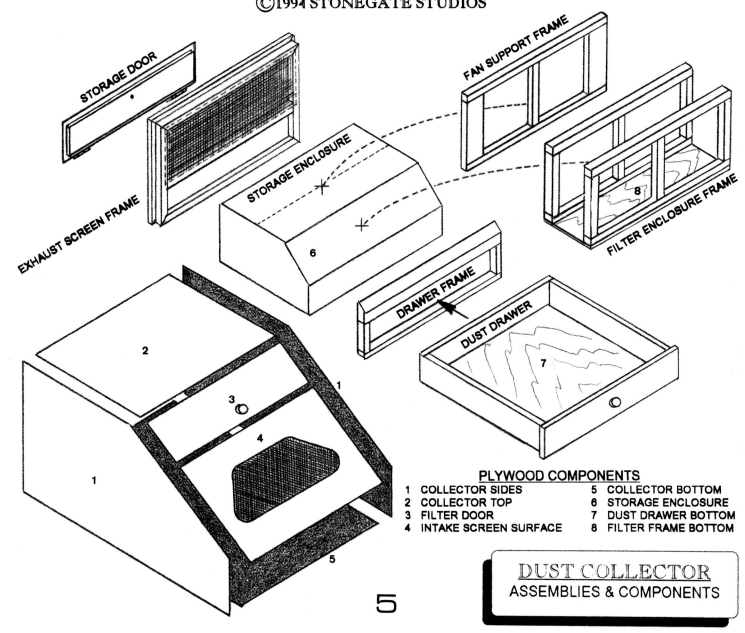

PLYWOOD COMPONENTS

1	COLLECTOR SIDES	5	COLLECTOR BOTTOM
2	COLLECTOR TOP	6	STORAGE ENCLOSURE
3	FILTER DOOR	7	DUST DRAWER BOTTOM
4	INTAKE SCREEN SURFACE	8	FILTER FRAME BOTTOM

DUST COLLECTOR
ASSEMBLIES & COMPONENTS

5

Dust Collector Assembly

STEP 1) Lay out a full scale finished side view of the dust box on a piece of poster board or cardboard taken from any cardboard box that is big enough. Layout all dimensions of the collector designing around the size of the filter you have chosen. *Plan the size of the filter holding brackets to a dimension that will hold the filter snugly enough so as not to allow air and dust to pass around the filter, but loosely enough to allow the filter to be removed for cleaning or replacement.*

STEP 2) Cut the 3/8" plywood sides to size. Make each side an exact duplicate of the other.

STEP 3) Cut the plywood bottom, top flat, and sloped front to size. *Decide where and how the switch/AC outlet box will be mounted, and make appropriate cutout.*

STEP 4) Layout and cut intake screen hole to desired size and shape in sloped front panel.

STEP 5) Filter enclosure — Assemble front and back filter frames, and attach plywood spacer piece to bottom of the frames, spacing frames to proper thickness to fit filter. *Make sure enough space has been left to allow a snug fit for the filter, but will still allow filter to be taken in and out with ease.*

STEP 6) Storage enclosure — Assemble enclosure as per sketch — make sure storage enclosure and filter enclosure assemblies are exactly the same width.

STEP 7) Assemble intake screen frame, exhaust screen frame, dust drawer frame and fan support frame of 3/4" stock. *Support frame for fans can be a solid piece of plywood with round holes slightly larger than the diameter of the fan blades. This type of support frame seems to make optimum use of air flow.*

STEP 8) Attach filter enclosure assembly to storage enclosure assembly as shown on side view of plan.

STEP 9) Position and assemble plywood collector sides to filter/storage assemblies. *Check the assembly by taking the filter in and out several times to insure that it can be easily placed and replaced.*

STEP 10) Attach plywood bottom to collector.

STEP 11) Install fan support frame, exhaust screen frame, and dust drawer frame.

STEP 12) Mount fan(s) in fan support frame.

STEP 13) Attach the plywood top flat to collector.

STEP 14) Mount outlet box, wire fan(s) to switch, and switch/outlets to power cord. *Choose a heavy duty power cord and make sure entire circuit is properly grounded all the way to the plug!*

STEP 15) Assemble a 3/4" frame to the shape of (and about 1/2" bigger all the way around than) the opening of the intake screen hole. Cut 1/4" wire mesh* to the size of the outer dimensions of the screen frame, and attach hardware cloth to frame with small electrical staples. Fit screen/frame to intake opening from the underside, and attach with appropriate length screws* from top, sandwiching screen between plywood and 3/4" frame.

STEP 16) Assemble dust drawer to appropriate length, width, and depth, attach drawer pull, and slide drawer into place. *Drawer must be accurately dimensioned to fit snugly against rear of storage enclosure wall below filter, as well as back of drawer face fitting snugly against drawer frame opening.*

STEP 17) Attach filter and storage access doors using hinges and pulls of choice. Storage access door is attached to screen guard frame prior to screen guard frame installation. *No door catch is necessary for the filter access door, and spring loaded hinges were used for the storage access door.*

STEP 18) Attach 1/4" wire mesh to back side of screen guard frame with electrical staples, and install frame assembly to front of fan compartment. *Use screws to attach frame with no glue, as the removal of this frame is necessary to access, service, or replace fans.*

MACHINE HANGER

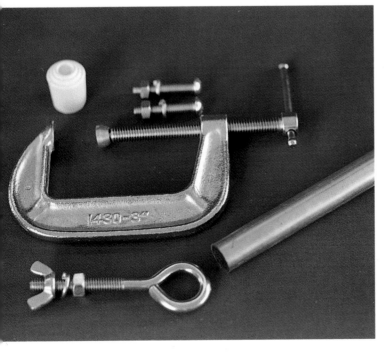

Parts List

1 3" C-clamp,
2 1/4" x 1 1/2" Round/Head bolts & nuts
1 32" length of metal electrical conduit (about 3/4" outside diameter)
1 5/16" x 5" Eye-bolt
1 5/16" nut (stop nut for eye-bolt)
1 5/16" wing nut
1 5/8" rubber leg cap

Construction

STEP 1) Cut the piece of 1/2" conduit to a 32" length. *Length will depend on the placement of a holder for the handpiece, distance of machine from operator, and height of bench top from the floor, but 32" seems to be a good all around length.*

STEP 2) Drill two holes large enough to accept the 2 1/4" round head bolts, three inches apart in the handle/body of the C-clamp.

STEP 3) Drill two matching holes through the conduit three inches apart and starting 1 1/2" up from the bottom end of the conduit.

STEP 4) Drill one hole large enough to accept the 5/16" eye bolt through the conduit at 1 1/2" down from the upper end of the conduit, facing in the direction the machine is to hang.

STEP 5) Thread 5/16" nut on eye bolt about 1/2" beyond thickness of the conduit, put through hole, and bind tightly to conduit with lock washer and wing nut.

STEP 6) Assemble C-clamp tightly to conduit with 1/4" nuts, lock washers, and bolts.

STEP 7) Push rubber leg cap on upper end of conduit. *The cap is optional, but I like the looks and the safety aspect.*

CAROUSEL BIT ORGANIZER

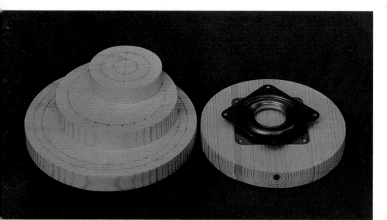

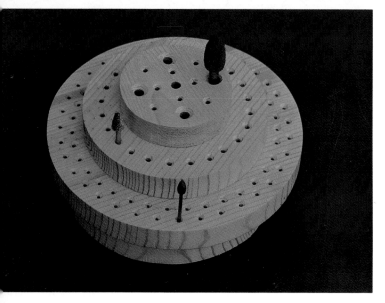

Parts List

1 small lazy Susan bearing
1-5 graduated circular plates and base of 3/4" clear pine, hardwood or plywood.

The carousel shown has a 7" base and bottom plate diameter. The upper plates are graduated by two inches less in diameter. *Circular base and plates are preferred, because square units have a tendency to catch on items that have been placed in the way of their rotation.*

Construction

STEP 1) Layout rings for bit shank holes on plates with a compass. The top plate will have rings all the way to the center, and the lower rings will each have one or two outer rings.

STEP 2) Space individual hole locations around and along the rings with a pair of dividers, pushing divider points into wood to leave location mark and drill tip guide.

STEP 3) Drill holes at hole locations around the rings to accept the size (or combination of sizes) for the bit shanks used. Drill all holes to 5/8" **maximum depth — don't go through the bottom of the plates.** *The shank sizes for bits shown and used throughout this book are 3/32", 1/8", and 1/4" —use drills only slighty larger than this to easily remove and replace bits in holes while carving.*

STEP 4) Round or shape upper edges of plates with router. (optional)

STEP 5) Stack and attach plates.

STEP 6) Stain or finish carousel plates and base as desired. *Don't fill the bit holes with finish. Usually a light coat with a stain/lacquer combination is sufficient.*

STEP 7) Mount lazy susan bearing between plates and base.

STEP 8) Mount or leave free standing on work surface

ACCESSORY TRAY/TRAVEL BOX

Parts List

1 **3" depth** plastic refrigerator storage box with self-sealing cover
1 3/4" clear pine, hardwood, or plywood stock to fit bottom of plastic box
1 or more plastic soap dishes with covers
1 drawer pull knob

Construction

STEP 1) Make a cardboard template that will fit the bottom of the plastic box. Size it to allow easy removal and replacement in the box.

STEP 2) Transfer shape of cardboard template to 3/4" wood stock and cut to size. Smooth edges, and test fit to box until wooden plate can be removed and replaced with ease.

STEP 3) Layout and drill bit shank holes in desired locations.

STEP 4) Mount drawer pull knob in center of wooden plate for removal handle.

STEP 5) Mount accessory soap dish box(es) in desired locations.

PVC PIPE TOOL HOLDERS

HANDPIECE CRADLE

Parts List

1" (Inside diameter) PVC pipe. *Each cradle is 4" long, and each 4" length makes two cradles.*

Construction

STEP 1) Cut the pipe to a 4" length using band saw, hack saw, or PVC saw.

STEP 2) Cut the pipe in half along it's length.

STEP 3) Round the edges from bottom to top with band saw, rasp, or other suitable tool.

STEP 4) Smooth and round edges by hand or machine sanding.

STEP 5) Drill one or two countersunk holes in bottom of cradle.

STEP 6) Mount in desired location on work surface with 1" flat head wood screws.

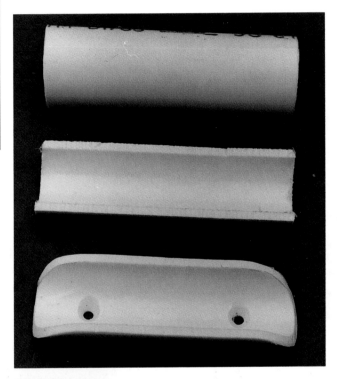

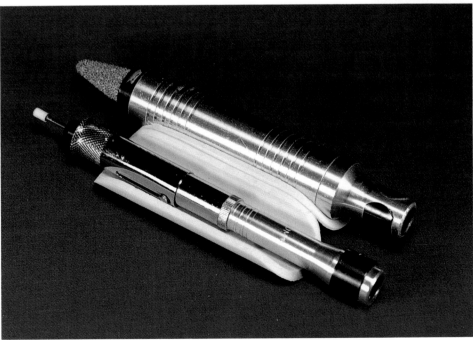

HANDPIECE HOLDER CUP

Parts List

3/4" (Inside diameter) rigid PVC electrical conduit with belled end.

Construction

STEP 1) Cut 7" to 8" off the belled end of the PVC conduit.

STEP 2) Cut both ends (bell and body) at matching 45 degree angles.

STEP 3) Round inside and outside edges of bell with rotary sander, file, or sandpaper.

STEP 4) Position holder as it will stand; drill a countersunk hole through the upper side of the 45 degree angle base cut.

STEP 5) Attach to work surface with 1 1/8" flat head screw. *Make sure that the bottom of the 45 degree cut remains flush with the work surface while the screw is being tightened.*

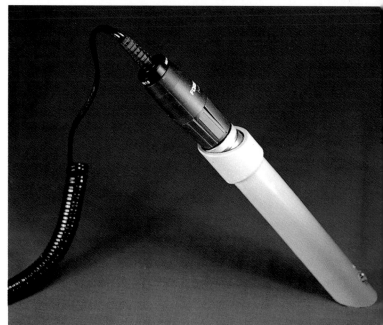

HANDPIECE HANGER CUP

Parts List

1/2" PVC pipe cap

Construction

STEP 1) Drill a 1/2" hole through the bottom center of the cap.

STEP 2) Cut in to the width of the hole at approximately a 10 degree angle from each side of the hole width with a bandsaw or hacksaw. Allow just enough room for the flex shaft to be placed and replaced from the cup as the handpiece is supported by the cup bottom.

STEP 3) Drill a countersunk hole about half way up at the back of the cap, opposite the center of the cut.

STEP 4) Slightly flatten the back surface of the cup beneath the countersunk drill hole with a file or sanding disc to assure a steady mounting to a bench or the side of a work surface.

STEP 5) Mount with a 1" flathead screw.

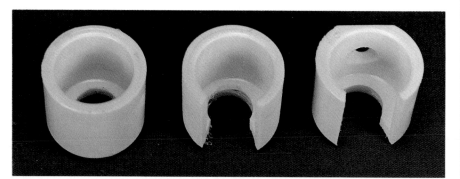

There are certain manual tools that I keep within easy reach at all times. Though I am first and foremost a power carver, I love quiet times in the forest or on a beach with my three most preferred hand tools — a knife and two chisels. These tools always go into my belt pack when I'm in the woods or swamps watching animals.

When I'm in the studios, and I need a knife to clean out a corner I can't reach, I want one that performs the way *I* want it to.

As I travel throughout the United States and Canada, I often meet knife makers, and have begun to collect carving knives wherever I find them. Recently, in Spring Hill, Florida, I met Rich Notto, a knife maker who manufactures one of the keenest cutting blades for a carving knife that I have yet to use.

Rich invented a Flex Strop ™ that makes sharpening a joy due to the ease it takes to bring my knives back to desired sharpness.

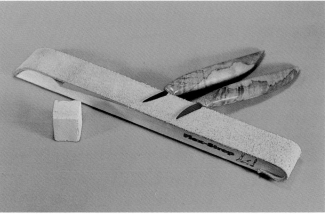

The two chisels I prefer are a deep straight parting tool (V-gouge), and the other, a deep straight U-gouge. I like to choke up on a chisel when I use it by hand, so I buy the best (not necessarily the costliest) straight handled chisels I can find, and cut the handles down to about three inches in length. This way they lend themselves exactly to my method of carving.

I now own four Notto knives, and they all satisfy criteria that I prefer in a knife before I'll use it, and not just add it to my collection. The handle has to fit comfortably and shift easily in my hand, the blade has to afford a medium to long reach, and the blade has to be thin and tapering with a flat bottom cutting edge. In addition, it has to be of a quality steel that will hold an edge, yet allow the edge to be easily reclaimed by stropping.

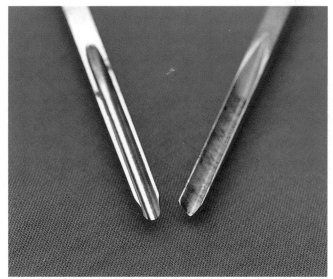

TOOL AND MATERIAL QUALITY

In my painting instructions, I suggest that the craftsman purchase the very best brushes that he or she can afford. This suggestion applies to the purchase of tools and materials to carve with as well. I seldom find second or third best quality in a tool (or most anything) to be acceptable in the long run. It's less time consuming, more satisfying, and easier to create with a tool or medium that you feel trust and confidence in. If you don't have to worry about the tool staying sharp, a power tool running intermittently, or wood that is punky, it's easier to give full attention to whatever you are creating.

It's much like having to make a long road trip with the engine of your car acting up. Chances are you won't be enjoying the scenery or the company half as much as you would if you knew the engine was running properly.

Aliphetic resin wood glue — I use aliphetic resin glues where a glue-up for a blank over a large area is needed. I prefer this type of glue for seams (when and if I have to have a seam) over longer areas that I will be carving such as along the animal's back or stomach. I find that this type of joint, when glued up and clamped with reasonable pressure, is easier to carve and texture without showing a seam mark. Further, it doesn't as adversely effect the sharpness of knives, chisels, or rotary bits as do some other glues. *The type used by the author is manufactured by Borden, Inc. of Columbus, Ohio and found in hardware and building supply stores.*

Epoxy glue — I use only the 5-minute set variety of this glue for everything that I do. If a head has to be attached in a position that requires it to be used as a separate piece from the body, it's a simple matter, even for someone as impatient as I am, to hold the pieces together with enough pressure by hand until the glue sets. *The 5-minute type used by the author is manufactured by Devcon Corp. of Danvers, Massachusetts and found in hardware and building supply stores.*

Epoxy paste — As the name implies, this product has the consistency of paste (think of toothpaste) when mixed. I can't imagine being without it for finish shaping antlers, fills, and repairs. I broke the tip off the beak of a Kestrel that I was carving, and subsequently lost the piece that broke off. I built the tip back up using epoxy paste, shaped it with saliva covered fingertips, and restored the lost section with virtually no shaping left to do. *See Making Metal Antler Sets.*

Epoxy putty — Another A + B ™ epoxy mix, but with the consistency of modeling clay. I use epoxy putty to set the eyes and to model the eyelids on my animals. *See Setting Glass Eyes.*

I also use it where the occasional small fill and modeling job is needed for repairs.

— A + B WOOD WORKS ™ is an excellent bonding and mending medium that has a wood-like appearance and can be shaped, modeled, sanded and textured. *The manufacturer says it can even be threaded which could come in handy for base mountings. I haven't had occasion to test this aspect of it yet.*

At the time of this writing, the only retailer I know that sells the A + B epoxy paste and puttys described and used in this book is Craftwoods Supply, in Timonium, Maryland. The manufacturer is the Hexel Corporation in Chatsworth, California, and east coast distribution is through Bautz Associates, 143 Tilford Rd, Somerdale, New Jersey.

III CARVING TECHNIQUES

STROKE VARIATIONS

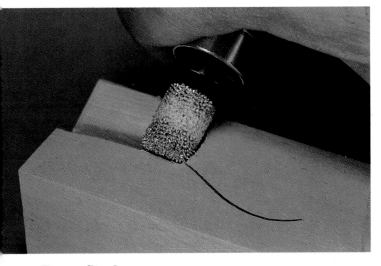

Brace Stroke

— the handpiece is brought towards the braced thumb. Used with larger coarse bits where a power stroke is required to remove or waste away stock. The thumb is braced against any convenient part of the carving and used to control the amount of power needed to maintain stability and regulation of the stroke for shaping.

Drag Stroke

— handpiece is held like a pencil and the stroke executed (usually along a pencilled guideline) in the same manner one would draw a pencil line from top to bottom of paper. Probably the most used stroke of all to relieve away a desired area or mass for shaping.

Since the **drag stroke** is the one stroke used for about ninety percent of relieving and shaping, and the **flame-shaped bit** is the bit used for about ninety percent of relieving and shaping, it will be most beneficial to learn to use the following variations of the drag stroke:

High Angle (Drag Stroke)

— when the handpiece (with flame-shaped bit) is held at a high degree of angle, the resultant cut is a V cut, very much the same as the cut of a V-gouge or parting tool.

Shaping Stroke

— handpiece is held like a pencil and the stroke is executed from side to side in the same manner as one would erase a pencil mark. Handpiece is usually held at a low angle while the bit is removing stock or shaping.

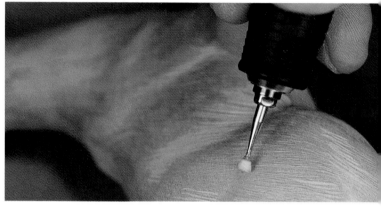

Low Angle (Drag Stroke)

— when the handpiece (with flame-shaped bit) is held at a low degree of angle, the resultant cut is a U-cut, very much the same as the cut of a U-gouge.

Texturing Stroke

— handpiece is held like a pencil and the stroke is executed from side to side in a zig-zag motion. Handpiece is held in a high angle position so that just the corner of the bit meets the stock, giving a fine deep hair-like cut. Cylindrical or inverted cone shaped stone bits are preferred for this operation.

MENTAL REQUIREMENTS

Beyond selection of proper tools and materials, we find the next three most important requirements to the completion of any carving.

Subject Knowledge, Carving Skill, and Desire.

What makes carving difficult?
Why can't everyone/anyone carve?
Why isn't the result as imagined?

All three questions have the same three answers —

Lack of:
Subject Knowledge
Carving Skills
Desire

I am fond of telling new students, "if you can sit up and breath at the same time, you can learn to carve". The process of learning is little, when compared to the necessities of desire, subject knowledge, and skills. Without a blending of the three, carving derives little satisfaction.
If you don't know your subject, carving skills and desire are limited or useless.
If you haven't developed skills, subject knowledge and desire is useless.
If you haven't the desire, skill or knowledge is limited.

Subject Knowledge — You want to carve a horse. No matter how skilled you are, or how great your desire, you can't carve a proper horse if you don't know the physical, structural, and finite details of a horse.

Carving Skills — You want to carve a horse. No matter how much you know about horses, or how great your desire, you can't carve a proper horse if you haven't developed and mastered basic carving skills.

Desire — You don't want to carve a horse, but have to, for some reason beyond your control. No matter how skilled or knowledgeable, if you are unwilling, or don't care about doing it, the result and enjoyment of your craft, will never be what it would be if you put yourself wholeheartedly into the project.

An example of the above might be a hypothetical situation where you have to choose and financially support one of three golfers, each with the same set of clubs, each with equal skill and knowledge of the course, however:
one would rather be fishing, but has to give it a try because he's in debt,
one resents having to prove himself, and could win if **only** he had a better set of clubs,
and one just loves to play, and revels in the game with no thought of having to win.
Which one is the obvious choice?

IV ANIMAL CARVING

Layout Considerations

1) **Consider** the direction of grain that will give the greatest amount of strength to the overall piece. If the completed piece has a weakness such as grain running across a leg, or an ear, or a beak, in time through shipping, showing, dusting, or handling of any kind, it will get broken. It is difficult to justify the repair of a higher priced carving because the craftsman never considered the consequence of weak areas on the piece, or worse, took an easier, quicker way out during the layout process.

2) **Consider** whether it would be stronger and easier to carve the piece if various sections were glued up, rather than attempting to carve the piece from a single block layout.

3) **Consider** whether the piece is to be a part of several free standing elements. How might it gain from, or lend strength to, these other elements? *For example, you want a group of deer jumping over a fence or log, and wish to give the piece a look of action with some of the deer appearing to be suspended in air and as unsupported as possible.*

4) **Consider** how much handling the piece will undergo throughout its lifetime. If the carving has to be shipped across the country, will it withstand the pressures of handling that it must undergo to get there? An agent for one of the leading parcel carriers that I use once told me that any package I send should be able to withstand a drop from waist-high. Having watched how some air freight and surface delivery folks handle packages, I give this rule of thumb much consideration during the layout stage, and continue to do so during the entire carving process.

5) **Consider** placement of grain for ease of carving. If the end grain is going to fall in an area of high exposure and high detailing, to facilitate strength and ease of carving, you may want to arrange the layout so that a side or cross grain falls in this area once the piece is blanked out.

The considerations given are but a few, and each carving will present new and different challenges to approach and consider. Give these concerns the attention they deserve during the planning stage; save yourself difficulty and anguish during the carving stages.

Project Sequence

A carving must be planned in much the same way as a trip is planned. If you want to go to Banff National Park, you can't just jump in a car and drive off. Drive off to where? Do you know the direction, the distance, climatic conditions, the route numbers, the cost of travel, hotels, or food? A trip must be planned for in advance, with allowances made for unplanned contingencies. The same applies to the planning of a carving — there is a logical sequence to the conclusion of any carving.

The ensuing terms are given to provide a general, but sequential, progression to the planning of a carving. The sequence may fit your need as it stands, or you may want to expand or reduce some areas to better suit your manner of carving.

Idea/Image — whatever the carving, it first begins as an idea and/or image in your mind. The trick is to get the image out of your mind through a two-dimensional plane to the third dimension.

Drawing/Sketch — once the image is drawn on a piece of paper, it can be manipulated, changed, drawn and redrawn to the satisfaction of its originator.

Template — serves as a guide to cutting the carving blank. If several carvings are to be done from the same drawing, a more permanent outline is cut from cardboard or other templating material. If the carving is to be a one-time effort, then the drawing can be glued directly to the block and cut from there.

Block — selection of a suitable block of wood for the carving project is extremely important. Considerations such as size, grain direction, dryness of wood, hardness/workablilty, and beauty are all major concerns to the selection and cutting of a carving blank.

Size is a consideration if the carving can't be laminated — usually the case if the carving is not painted, and is to have a natural finish.

Grain direction is important to the planning of carving strength. If a thin cross-grained area is left to support a large mass without internal support, the carving will break somewhere during or after completion leaving extra work, cost, and usually an unhappy customer.

Dryness must be considered not so much before and during, but after the carving is completed. It's disheartening to finish an intricate carving only to have it check or split due to contraction caused by moisture evaporation.

Hardness/workability of the wood chosen to carve is a prime consideration to the convenience and comfort enjoyed as one carves. Some hardwoods will require totally different carving techniques and time than would softer woods of the same size. Workability of wood within the same species will also vary greatly. For example, I have carved pieces of basswood, tupeloe, and even jelutong that have ranged from extremely hard and brittle, to perfectly suitable, to so punky as to resemble open grained balsa wood — sometimes within the same piece of wood.

Beauty — if the carving is to be left with natural finish (grain exposed), consideration must not only be given to the direction of grain for strength of the carving, but placed properly within the carving to exemplify the beauty of the grain to its fullest. If the carving is to be finish painted, then the prime consideration to direction of grain is for strength to the carving.

Blank — the carving blank is an outline shape of the proposed carving, that has been cut two ways from a carving block — usually cut from the front view and one of the side views on a band saw.

Rough Shape — rough shaping is nothing more than removing or hogging out all obvious areas of undesirable stock such as bringing a head and/or body to approximate width, or the removal of stock from between legs, or unwanted overhangs. The blank will have a very square appearance at this time, but will possess the beginnings of the carving's final shape.

Rounded Rough Shape — each area of the roughed square shapes are rounded to approximate the final dimensions of the finished carving. This is the point at which many beginning carvers fail, due to lack of confidence or subject knowledge, simply by not removing enough of the squared portion and bringing it to a properly rounded shape. This is evident by the "squarish" looking carvings presented by new or unknowledgeable woodcarvers at carving shows or displays.

Contoured or Refined Shape — when the carving has been given a general rounded shape, each particular rounded shape must then be contoured and/or refined to a final shape in preparation to accept final detailing and texturing. For example, the rounded shape of the muscle mass of a horse's flank would be contoured to show the depressions between the major muscles that show from beneath the skin.

Detailed Shape — once the carving has been contoured with all the appropriate "humps and hollows", any additional detail is given to a particular area in its turn. These detailed shapes can be anything from a flexed muscle, or a lip curl, to a separated hair mass, or the wave and flow of a tail or mane.

Textured Shape — each shape is textured with hair or fur characteristic of its location on the animal. Consideration must be given to scale as well as the length, coarseness, and type of hair that would be found on a particular animal. Short, light overlapping texture lines would represent the fine hair on a bear's muzzle, whereas heavy, deeper overlapping texture lines would represent the coarse hair found on its shoulders and back.

Finished Shape — paint will further add to the enhancement of the carving. The raises and hollows of the contours can be shaded and highlighted to give greater detail and depth to the carving's appearance. Hair splits, overlays, and curls can be shaded and highlighted to give an even finer but deeper detail. As necessitates, this may be one of the woodcarver's last chances to fool the eye of the observer.

CARVING SEQUENCE

When I began carving, I had to develop a sequential method to follow because I would often find myself recarving areas and details I had completed, but had to be wiped out as part of a nearby shaping process. What follows is a general overview of the sequence I follow when I carve. I say general overview, because depending on the animal I'm carving, or even the mood I'm in, I rarely carve from start to finish the same way twice, and this arrangement allows me that latitude.

A) Rough shape, contour, and detail shape animal.
   See Carving the Head and Body
B) Finish shape ears, nose/nostrils, mouth, and/or fangs or teeth.
   See Carving the Ear
   See Carving the Nose & Nostrils
   See Carving the Mouth & Teeth
C) Finish shape the tail and/or mane.
   See Carving Hair Overlays and Separations
D) Finish shape hooves or paws/claws.
   See Carving Hooves, Paws, & Claws
E) Finish carving or setting the eyes.
   See Carving the Eye
   See Setting Glass Eyes
F) Texture entire animal.
   See Texturing Hair, Tails, & Manes
G) Carve or fabricate, fit, and set horns or antlers.
   See Making antlers and horns
H) Apply finish

The above is a suggested sequence for carving an animal — it may be advantageous to your method of carving to rearrange the sequence.

The Head

The first most distinctive thing about an animal carving is the head. If the head you have carved on your tiger doesn't look like a tiger's head, even though you have painted or textured a nice striped tiger pattern on the body, the whole carving has lost credence.

You must observe and familiarize yourself with the head before you can carve an acceptable likeness. If a live example is not available, then knowledge must be gained through references such as photographs, drawings, and/or video tapes.

Once you have the references, you must then learn to extract the visual knowledge you need to enable you to visualize what you will carve.

When I first began to carve, I started with birds, and at the time I had neither State or Federal permit to have birds (alive or dead) in my possession to study, so it was extremely difficult. A good friend and exceptional bird carver from Toronto, Canada taught me to "read" photographs of songbirds to gain the knowledge I needed to lay out, shape, and detail any species of bird right down to the feather groups including individual feathers. I remember his exasperation when he told me to look at a particular photo and tell him what I saw. When I interpreted my observations, he said, "You see everything, yet you see nothing!"

Although I have modified what he taught me, the method remains the same, and I think of Bob every time I'm "pulling" shape and detail from an animal's head.

First, observe the head not as whole, but by views:
from the front, side, top, and bottom,
one at a time, memorize the outer shape of each view,
break the view into separate distinctive shapes or areas,
note the shape, contouring, and fine detail of one area
see how it joins and blends with or into the next distinctive shape or area,

carefully address every shape or area within a view,
then look at the whole head.

You will soon note many similarities from animal to animal — that most animals have the same likeness but differently shaped. So much so, that I use the format that follows for all animals when I study the head from the front:
— the width and shape of the frontal bone or the space between the eyes,
— the shape and contour of the forehead and the space between the ears,
— the contour, width, and length of the nasal or "muzzle" bone that runs from a point above the nostrils upward into the frontal bone,
— the size, shape, and location of the eye brow (protuberance caused by the brow bone above the eye),
— the size and extent of the lid pouch immediately below the eye (some call it a tear pocket because in a human, its the part that swells with prolonged or intensive crying).

Develop a study format that suits you and you will soon find yourself looking at everything you wish to carve in a totally different manner. A manner that at the very least, instills confidence and greater joy in what you want to do.

When the head is laid out on carving stock from a pattern or drawn directly on the stock, give thought to how the grain will be running through it as a finished carving. The obvious way to gain as much strength as possible is to run the grain in the direction the muzzle is pointing. But on a long eared animal such as a rabbit, mule deer, or a donkey, how will that grain direction effect the strength of the ears? Perhaps the ears can be strengthened somewhat by rotating the pattern to a point where the grain direction is more evenly distributed between the ears and the muzzle.

24

Body Structure and Shape

You must have a general idea of the muscle structure and shape of the animal you are carving. Learn where the individual muscles are located and their shape. Any animal anatomy book can give you the general shape of the individual muscles, the size with respect to other muscles, and how all the muscles lay together to form a particular mass.

Knowledge of how the muscles lay under the skin, will aid greatly in establishing the shape that is characteristic to the animal being carved.

Build a pictorial reference folder for the animal you choose to carve. If the animal is a wild species, hunting/outdoor magazines, nature/wildlife books, and calenders are all excellent sources for references.

I have found the best source to be a zoo or game farm, if the caged animal will cooperate. Most of the time, zoo keepers or attendants are most helpful when you explain why you want photos that are not run-of-the-mill pictures.

Photograph the highest degree of detail you can get, both general and specific. Create a checklist of general questions like:

What instantly tells me what this animal is?
What is the shape and mass of the entire body?
What are the characteristics of the body?
What are the characteristics of the head?
How does the head compare to the neck?
How does the neck compare to the shoulders?
How do the shoulders compare to the back and stomach?
How does the back compare to the hindquarters?
Is this animal a predator or a prey species?
How does it survive? Does it run? Does it attack?
What is the overall quality of the fur?
What are the differences between this animal and others of the same
   species?

Next, pursue more specific questions about the animal you want to carve. If you plan to carve a bear and you don't know exactly what a bear's eye looks like, try to get a shot of just an eye. Fill the whole frame with just an eye.

Ask yourself specific questions like:
What's the difference between a bear's eye and a deer's eye?
How are the nostrils on a bear shaped?
How does the upper lip tie into the nostrils?
What does the corner of a bear's mouth look like and where is it
   located?
How does the hair on the muzzle and head compare to hair on the
   withers?
How many toes and claws are exposed on each paw?
How long are the claws on a particular species of bear?
Are the front claws longer than the rear claws?
Does the shape of a front paw differ from the shape of a rear paw?
How about the bear's tail?

Review the carving sequence in your mind before you begin gathering reference detail, and it will soon become very apparent how little or how much you know about the overall appearance and individual details found on the animal you are about to carve. The more detailed reference material you have, the easier and more enjoyable the carving process and experience.

Body Basics

In my book, **CARVING REALISTIC FACES WITH POWER**, I talk about how all human ears are the same, but each one is different, even on the same head. As such, all animal bodies are the same, yet each is different from species to species. Since the body trunk is the largest area on an animal, it's the easiest place to start.

Every body trunk includes the front quarters (shoulders and front legs), the mid-section (back, sides, & belly), and the rear quarters (hips and hind legs). Once we realize that the basic bone structure is the same for all animals, then "plugging in a shape" is easy. Just assign a suitable body shape, then add a properly shaped and proportionate neck, head, legs, and tail, and you should have a suitable representation of the desired animal.

How do we decide on a suitable body shape? First by generalization, then by comparison, and finally by distinctive features. For example, say we want to carve a black bear. We must determine the general shape of a bear's body. How do we do this? Hopefully, we have studied a reference subject, photos, and/or anything that is representative of the species of bear that we want to carve. Having done this, we know that a bear doesn't have the sloping back of giraffe, nor the center sag of a horse, nor the straight back of a cow. By this process of elimination, we can assign a general shape and proportion of the type of bear that we want.

Once we have a general shape:
How does it compare to the original?
What are the extremes within which our lay out must be confined?
If the animal is to be carved in a particular position, what happens to the muscles?
Will the thigh muscles be the same in a leaping pose as they would be in a standing pose?
If the animal is posed in a stretching leap, what happens to the back and the stomach?
Do they become smaller and elongated?
Do the ribs show?

Be relentless with your questioning at this stage, because once you have the carving blank cut out, it may be much too late to correct an oversight such as leaving too little stock in the hind quarters because you don't (or didn't!) understand how the muscles bulge before, during, or after a particular activity.

Carving the Head & Body

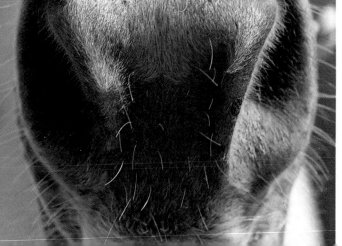

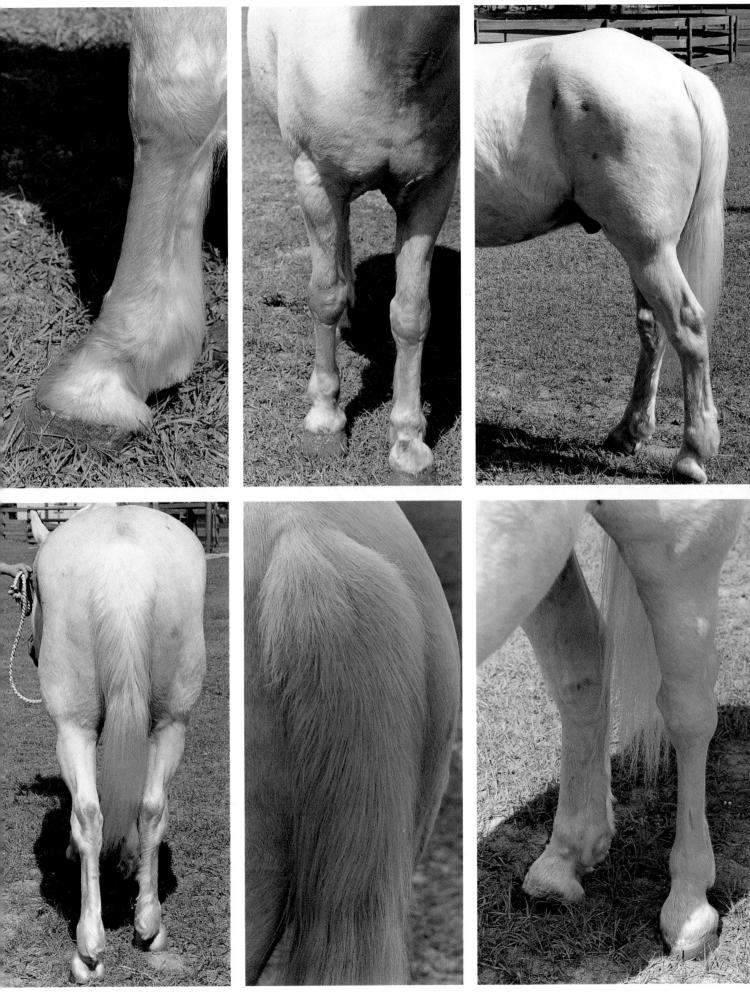

STEP 1) Surround yourself with references of the subject animal.

STEP 3) Cut out the side outline of the animal using a coping saw, jig saw, or bandsaw.

STEP 2) Draw the animal as you want it, or choose a prepared pattern and reposition the pose if you desire to do so. *See "A Lesson on Cheating" in my book,* **CARVING REALISTIC FACES WITH POWER.** Cut out a carboard template to trace around, or draw the outline directly on the carving wood.

STEP 4) If blank is a lay up (two or more pieces glued side by side), glue them up at this time.

STEP 5) Draw a centerline all the way around the carving blank, unless there is a glue line already there to serve as one.

STEP 6) If possible, cut out the top view of the animal to get rid of stock.

STEP 7) Waste away any stock possible using the bandsaw. *If you feel unsure as to how much stock to remove, or feel that* **this operation is dangerous,** *leave excess stock on the blank and remove it during the roughing out process.*

STEP 8) Begin rough shaping the blank with a flame-shaped or tapered Tungsten Carbide Burr. Remove all unwanted stock, bringing the blank to a general shape, without specific or detailed shapes.

STEP 9) With a flame or pear shaped ruby carver, begin refining individual areas on the body, such as the hips, stomach, shoulders, backbone, neck, head, back, and legs.

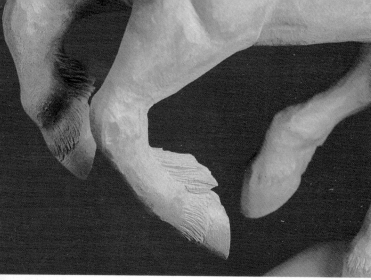

STEP 10) Refine the shapes of the individual areas:
A) Bring the legs to their final shape with tendons, hoof shapes, knee joints, and general muscle masses.
B) Shape the hip, stomach, and shoulder muscle masses.
C) Shape the back, neck, head, ears, and tail.
D) Define individual muscle masses as necessary. Example: if animal is running, jumping, set to spring, or just standing, the muscles will be indented, bulged, or stretched differently, requiring individual shaping.

STEP 11) On the head, relieve away and detail the eyes, ears, mouth/teeth, nose, nostrils, and hair masses with overlays and separations. *See the carving sequences that follow for a STEP-by-STEP illustration relevant to the feature or detail you want to carve.*

STEP 12) On the body, relieve away and detail hooves/paws, claws, manes, tails, capes, and all hair detail prior to texturing. *See the carving sequences that follow for a for STEP-by-STEP illustration relevant to the feature or detail you want to carve.*

STEP 13) Texture hair on the entire carving in areas that require hair. *See texturing hair.*

STEP 14) *Mount any antlers/horns not already a part of the carving. Glue antlers/horns in place, using as small an amount as necessary to get the job done, and taking care not to get epoxy glue on any part of the carving. Touch up and blend as necessary around the glued base(s).*

STEP 15) Seal the carving with a lacquer that preferably has a base compatible with the type of finish you plan to use. *Example: Use acrylic base lacquer for acrylic paints, and oil base lacquer for oil paints.*

Eyes

They say the eyes express everything. I don't agree with that statement one hundred percent — the eyes certainly give expression, but above all they give a carving the right characteristic. For example, it would be incorrect to carve the large, round, soft eyes of a deer on a wolf. Neither should the sharp, narrowed, triangular eyes of a wolf be found on a rabbit.

What makes the eye of a deer appear large, round, and soft?

What makes the eye of a wolf appear sharp, narrowed, and triangular?

The inside corner of the eye is lower than the outside corner on practically all animals. The eyes of **prey species** are more to the side of the head allowing for a greater field of vision, whereas the eyes of *predator species* are more forward with a more directional field of vision.

The eyes of the prey species are for the most part large and more rounded in appearance than the eyes of a predator, whose eyes appear smaller, elongated, and more triangulated with a lesser corner angle. The eyes of prey species also appear proportionately larger than do the eyes of a predator.

When I carve, I think of prey species eyes as being wider and more open to remain ever alert and aware of danger around and within a large area. Conversely, I think of the predator with narrowed eyes directed forward, with sight more inclined to a smaller area within which he has to "sight in" his prey, much as one would imagine tunnel vision to be. When coupled with the fact that the prey species eyes are located more to the sides of the head for greater peripheral vision, and the predator species eyes are located to the front of the head for a more directed vision, it makes sense that both evolved in the manner they have.

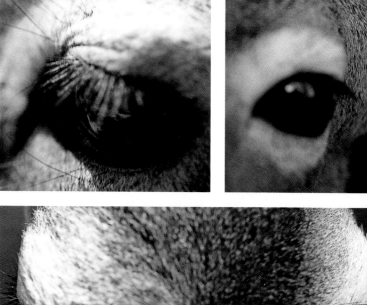

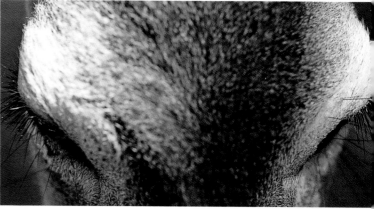

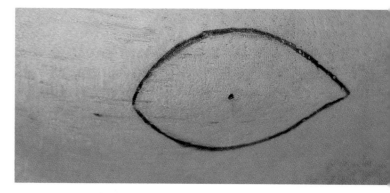

Carving the Eye

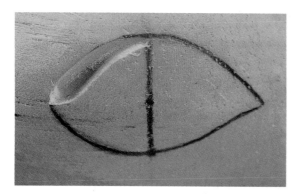

STEP 1) Prepare the mound or raised portion and surrounding area into which the eye will be carved. The mounds, raised areas, and head in general should be as symmetrical as possible.

STEP 2) Carefully lay out both eyes with pencil. The layout stage is critical to the finished size and location of the eyes, and overall symmetry of the head. Study the eye of the animal you are carving from any reference source that you can find, from a live animal to photos or sketches. *Be careful when using renditions that others have drawn. Some artists may not be accurate enough, or need the accuracy in their renditions that you might want in yours.*

STEP 3) Draw a line vertically through the center of each eye from lid to lid.

STEP 4) Make the first cut with a narrow flame-shaped ruby carver. Beginning at one corner of the eye, cut deeply with the tip of the bit, and draw along the upper eyelid to the centerline of the eye. The cut will become shallower as you draw away from the corner of the eye.

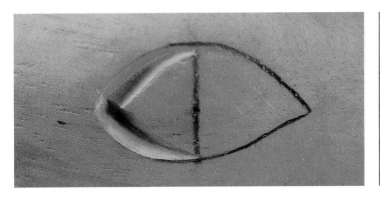

STEP 5) Now make a second cut starting within the same point as the first cut in the corner of the eye, and draw along the lower eyelid upwards to the centerline of the eye. Again, the cut will become shallower as you draw away from the corner of the eye to the centerline.

STEP 9) Starting at the exact point in the center of the eye, remove another triangular wedge that gets slightly deeper as it runs to the lower eyelid. The eyeball now has a very angular and faceted appearance.

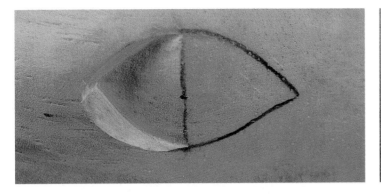

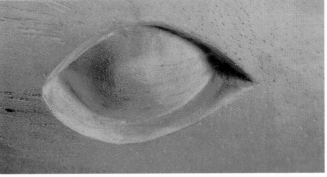

STEP 6) Cut out the stock between the upper and lower lids from the corner to the centerline. The area removed will be a wedge-shaped triangle.

STEP 10) Round out the eyeball exposed within the confines of the eyelids. Remember, the eyeball is spherical, while the eyelids and depressions around the eyelids will have a more ovate appearance.

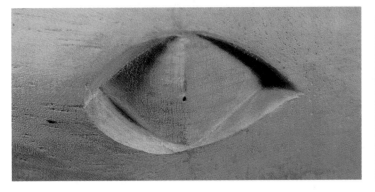

STEP 7) Repeat the same cuts starting at the opposite corner of the eye. The eye now has two triangular facets with a sharp ridge running through the middle.

STEP 11) Sharpen up any areas within the eye that need defining.

STEP 12) Define any lines that lead out of the corners of the eyes.

STEP 13) If the animal has a lid fold above the eye, carve it in and blend into surrounding area.

STEP 14) If the animal has a raised area below the eye, like the tear pouch on a human, shape and blend into surrounding area.

STEP 15) If you want a relieved pupil, draw the pupils on the eyes and relieve them out. Be sure the pupils are the same size and location on the eyes. You can spoil the appearance of the whole carving here. *Choose the correct shape of the pupil for the animal that you are carving — some have round, some elongated, and some, like cats and foxes, can have pointed ovals or spherical pupils.*

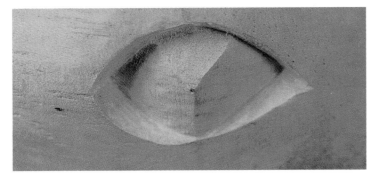

STEP 8) Starting from the exact center of the ridge through the middle of the eye, remove a triangular wedge that gets slightly deeper as it runs to the upper eyelid.

33

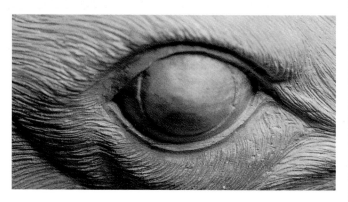

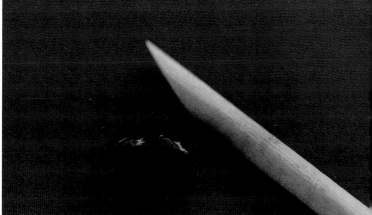

STEP 16) Prepare area around the eye for texturing.

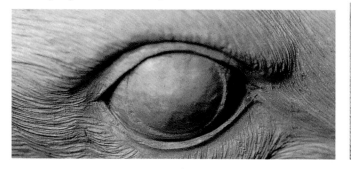

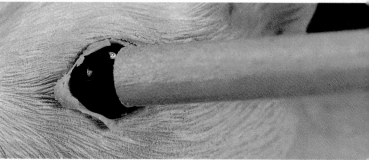

Setting a Glass Eye

STEP 1) Prepare the mound or raised portion and surrounding area into which the eye will be set. The mounds, raised area, and head should be as symmetrical as can be carved.

STEP 2) Locate the hole position for both eyes. Make a point at the exact center of the eye, and draw the extremes of the eye corners and lids. Around the center point, draw a circle slightly larger than the diameter of the glass eye to be used. *Use extreme care and accuracy, how the eyes are located now, not only determines how the finished eyes will appear, but will influence the overall appearance of the carving.*

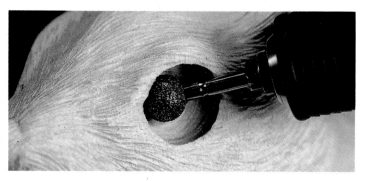

STEP 3) With a ball bit, begin at the very center dot, and with counterclockwise circular strokes, open the eye hole to a diameter slightly larger than the diameter of the glass eye to be used, and to a depth of about twice the front to back thickness of the glass eye.

STEP 4) Mix enough two-part epoxy putty to fill the eye hole to overflowing. Fill the eye to the top surface using a wiping stroke with the thumb that seats the putty firmly.

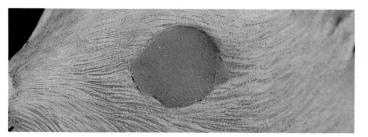

STEP 5) With the flat or slightly hollowed end of a dowel, seat the eye in the epoxy-filled hole. One-third of the diameter of the eye should protrude, with the pupil facing in the direction that you want the animal to appear to be looking. Most of the time it will suffice to install the eye with the pupil centered and the eye straight out. *Caution! If you want the pupils pointed in any direction other than centered and straight out, make sure they are both pointed and located symmetrically within the eyes in the direction you wish the animal to be looking. Any error here can give you a permanently cross eyed, lop eyed, and/or bug eyed animal.*

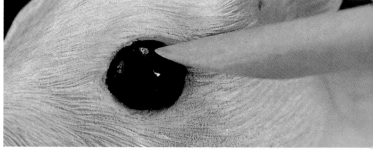

STEP 6) Trim the excess epoxy that squirts out around the eye as you push the eye in. With the flat of the wedge on your modeling tool, firm in and smooth the epoxy around the eye.

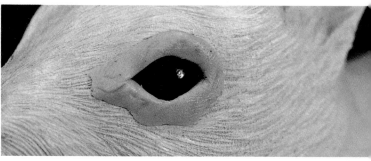

STEP 7) Make a small string or rope of epoxy by rolling a bit between the hands and lay a "bead" all the way around the eye.

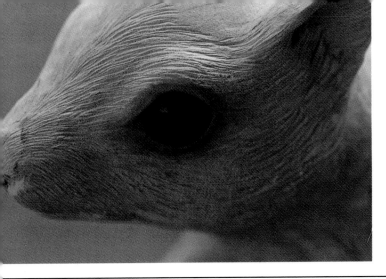

STEP 8) With the wedged end of the modeling tool, shape an eyelid from the epoxy laid around the eye. *Hint — keep the working end of the tool moist with water or saliva as you model, thus keeping the epoxy from sticking to the tool as you work. I am usually too lazy to get a glass of water to work from, so I stick the end of the modeling tool in my mouth to gain the moisture I need to prevent the epoxy from sticking. I have never had any ill effects, because the saliva never allows any epoxy to get stuck to the tool ... or my mouth!*

EARS

The ears of animals are highly mobile, perhaps more so in the prey species. Although ears may move independent of one another, (unless the carving is of a long-eared species such as a deer or rabbit) the carving will have a more suitable appearance if the ears are carved in symmetrical positions.

The ears are one indicator of attitude and purpose, for example, when a horse lays its ears back, it usually is angry and getting ready to bite. When a dog's ears go up its alerted to something. If I see a deer's ears waving I know its nervous and trying to locate a sound that it wants to identify before flight.

Observations for the ear:
— general shape of the ear
— base shape where attached to head
— shape of ear back
— tips of ears
— thickness of ear wall
— shape and extent of ear membrane
— depth of hollow inside ear
— how much of the bell or hollow is hidden by hair
— amount of hair inside ear
— direction and amount of hair on ear and away from ear base

For obvious reasons, the same points must be considered during the carving process. Astute observation and careful planning are required concerning the previous points. Obtain as many accurate and detailed references as possible to guide you through the planning and carving of animal ears.

Carving the Ear

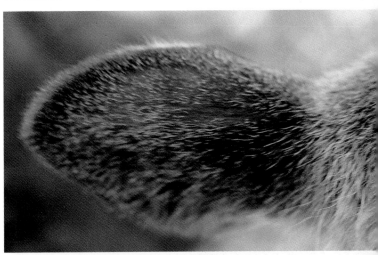

35

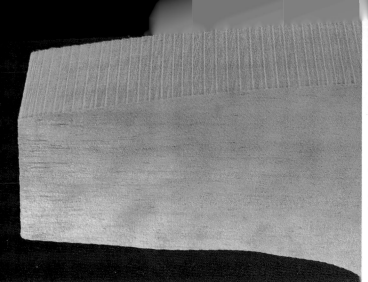

STEP 1) Block out the ears leaving enough stock to allow changes.

STEP 2) Establish the centerline of the head to allow symmetrical location of the ears with respect to the sides and center of the head.

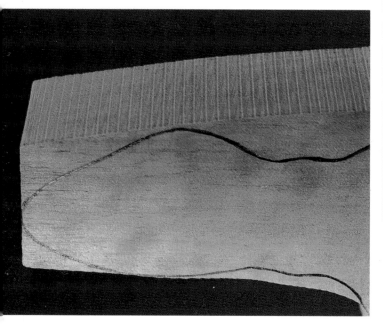

STEP 3) Sketch the general outline of the finished ears on blocked shape. Give the layout an "arm's length" look and decide if you are satisfied with the way you have the ears drawn. If anything seems amiss, erase and redraw.

STEP 4) Carve the outline shape of the ear. Leave the outline slightly larger than the desired finished outline of the ear.

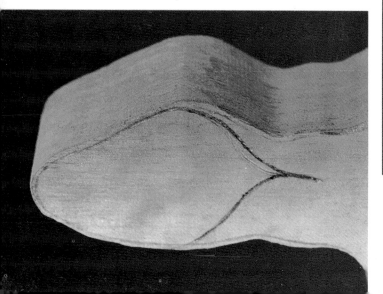

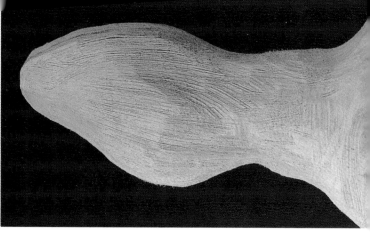

STEP 5) Using a flame-shaped or pear shape ruby carver, begin shaping the backside of the ear from the tip to the base. This is an easy place to go awry if too much stock is removed — especially from the tips of the ears.

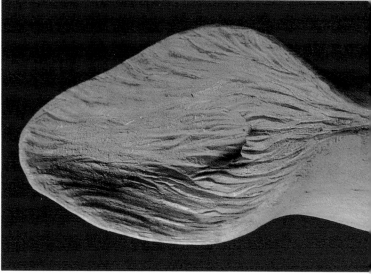

STEP 6) Using a flame-shaped ruby carver, begin shaping the inside of the ear by hollowing back to the wall of the ear. Work from the tip downward and inward, using care not to make the wall thinner than you want it, or worse, cut through the wall. As you work down to the base, don't cut away the area you have reserved for inner ear hair. This won't be a problem on animals with no inner ear hair, which will allow you to cut deeply into the ear cavity giving greater detail and depth to the carving.

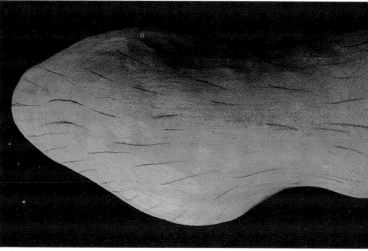

STEP 7) Shape and blend the base of the ear into the head, and prepare the area for texturing.

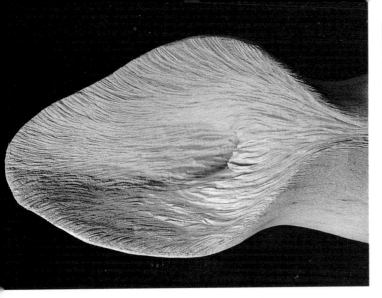

STEP 8) Finish shape the "tuft" of any existing inner ear hair, undercut where possible to give the appearance of depth and the ear cavity beneath. Retouch any areas of the ear that need to be brought to a finished shape.

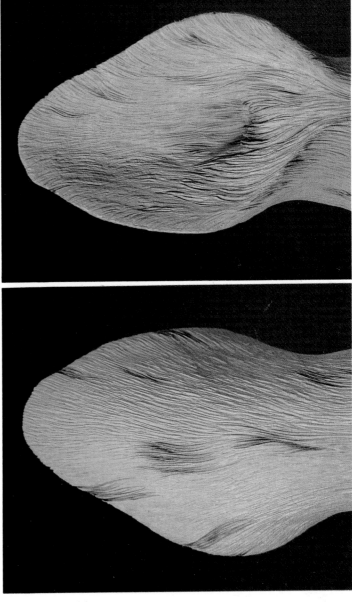

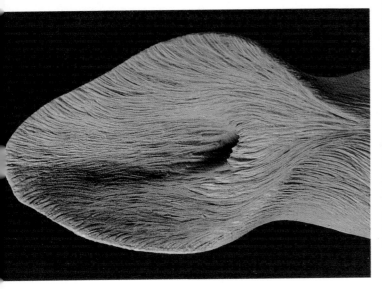

STEP 9) Texture the ear, blending the hair lines at the base of the ear into the direction of flow of hair coming from or going into, the back and head.

STEP 10) Woodburn any areas of coarse hair necessary to give depth of detail to the ear.

Nose

The human nose and some animal noses are amazingly alike in structure. If viewed from the side and tilted upwards about ninety degrees, its easy to see the similarities between a human nose and dog or bear nose. Often, as I wait for a plane or wait in a theater for the entertainment to begin, I observe the people around me, and I'm amazed at how easy it is to give them different animal features — or give their features to animals!

A common fault with noses found on many beginning carver's animals is that they haven't proper shape, or no shape at all. For some reason many carvers feel that a tapered snout with two pinholes will suffice, and go on to carve a highly accurate and detailed body leaving the poor animal to face the forever after with a nondescript proboscis.

First, look at the nose as a general shape, **without nostrils**. Observations for the nose:
— the shape(s) that will be required to carve this nose,
— the thickness of the nose to the lip line,
— how it blends into the lips,
— the width compared to the rest of the head,
— the length when compared proportionately to the rest of the head and body,
— the thickness from top to bottom,
— characteristics that make it prominent,
— features that makes this nose different from any other animal's nose,
— fineness or coarseness of hair leading off the nose,
— position the nose takes under different emotion such as anger, contentment, fear, etc. *For example, the nose of a dog or a bear turns upward when it snarls angrily, a cat's nose broadens as the cheeks pull back into a snarl, and the horse or moose nose seems to flatten as the nostrils flare before a bite or nip directed at the source of anger.*

37

Nostrils

The nostrils of most all animals (including man) have a common shape, that of opposing commas — ",". Although the opposing comma nostril openings are generally the same, the size and shape differs from species to species, and from animal to animal. Once you find the paired comma shapes you will find that bit of information leading you to the observation of other "commonalities". The gathering of small bits of data will keep increasing until what you couldn't "see" becomes second nature, allowing you an ever increasing storehouse of knowledge to use with your carving ability.

Study the animal you are carving for the exact configuration of these "common" nostril openings. If possible, take photos from various angles of the nostrils of the animal you wish to carve, if photography is out of the question, then surround yourself with every reference picture you can find, whether it is from a calender, a wildlife magazine, post card, or whatever you can find that has the animal's nose on it. Make folder files of all the data you have collected so you will have references for future projects.

One of the best reference medias I have found are the wildlife programs on television. I record them as they air (I now have close to one hundred), then when I plan to carve one of the animals I have in my video file, I run that tape and punch the pause button whenever I need a good long look at something like the nostrils. The nature channels are a bonanza for video reference filing. *A VCR with four recording heads is usually necessary to get a clear, unblemished stop frame (pause) that you wish to study for any length of time. I have actually traced outline sketches directly from the face of the television set on some of the more difficult animals that I didn't know well, or with which I felt insecure.*

Carving the Nose & Nostrils

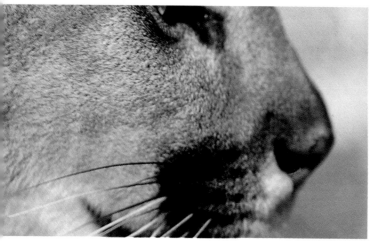

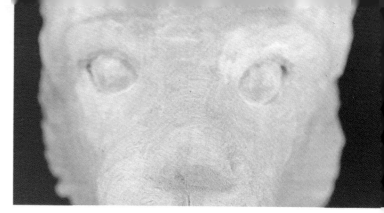

STEP 1) Make certain that the head, especially in the area of the muzzle, has been finish shaped. You can't carve a nose and nostrils into an area that hasn't been shaped to receive it. You can, but you will soon be carving a new nose to fit the final shape of the muzzle.

STEP 2) Lay out the nose pad symmetrically and with care. Note the extent of the pad from references and match your layout proportionately.

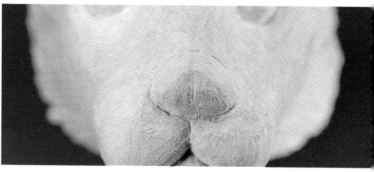

STEP 3) Shape the nosepad with a flame-shaped ruby carver, keeping in mind the position the nose pad should be in to portray action and emotion in the animal. *If you are carving an angry snarling bear, you want the nosepad turned up with nostrils flared, which will wrinkle the skin on top of the muzzle.*

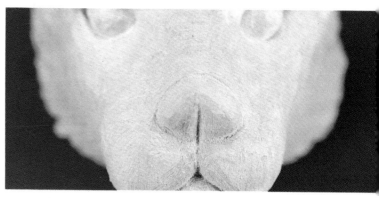

STEP 4) Relieve away the septum (the slot that runs from the upper lip upwards to terminate just between the nostrils, using a narrow flame-shaped ruby carver in a high angle position.

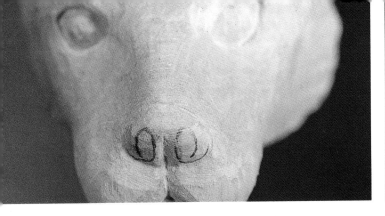

STEP 5) Draw a fine outline of the nostrils, keeping in mind any action or emotion of which the nose may be a part.

STEP 7) Carve and shape the tail of the comma with a small flame-shaped bit, making both nostril tails as symmetrical as possible.

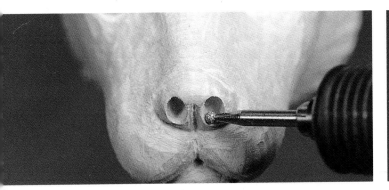

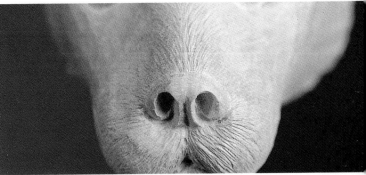

STEP 6) With a ball shaped ruby or diamond cutter (depending on size) stay within the body lines of the nostril comma and relieve a hole by starting in the middle and working around and down to shape the hole. Make the holes as symmetrical as possible for both nostrils.

STEP 8) Touch up the nose pad and nostrils as necessary, blending into upper lip, side, and top of muzzle in preparation for detailing of hair.

MOUTHS & TEETH

One of the strictest applications with regard to an animal's mouth is the simplest ... if you don't know what the inside of an animal's mouth looks like, don't carve it with an open mouth!

The mouth is rarely given careful scrutiny by the observer unless one or both of two instances occur. First, if the mouth is expressing an action or emotion and is meant to be a focal point, and/or second, if the mouth is incorrectly carved, and thereby draws attention.

I was judging the songbird category at a major exhibition, when the two other judges and I came upon a superbly carved meadowlark. The carver had the bird posed beautifully on a fence post with a vine curling along remnants of rusty barbed wire. The feather detailing and painting was as nice as we had seen of the hundred plus birds being judged. The bird had its head thrown back in a classic open mouthed meadowlark singing pose. However, when one looked into the mouth, the eye was greeted by an irregularly shaped hole painted black.

Competition was tight enough that the piece didn't take as much as an honorable mention. The carver later asked what "threw his bird out", and after we explained, he sheepishly admitted that he had no idea what the tongue or the inside of a meadowlark's mouth even looked like.

Closely study any references you have before you begin carving, so you have a concise idea. Note the following, and carve the mouth accordingly.

Carving the Closed Mouth

Observations for the closed mouth:
— the shape of the mouth and how it blends to the muzzle.
— the extent and prominence of the mouth.
— the shape and termination point of the mouth corners.
— the angle line between the lips of the closed mouth from front to back.
— the way the septum leads away from the upper lip to the nostrils.

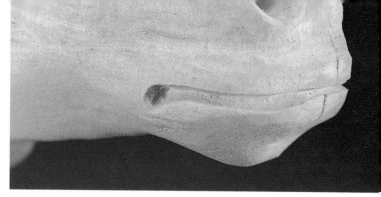

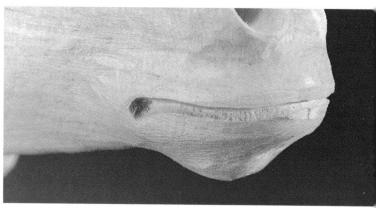

STEP 3) Shape the depressions made by the corners of the mouth (where upper and lower lip come together on either side of the muzzle.

STEP 4) Relieve away the thickness of lips and any indentations around the lips, blending back into the muzzle. *Leave enough stock to properly shape the septum and the extent of the nose pad.*

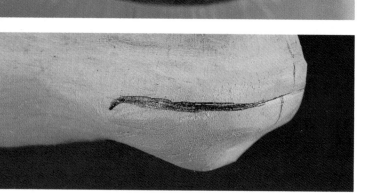

STEP 1) Draw the mouth exactly as you want it. *This is the most important STEP to relieving the mouth. Make your lines sharp and symmetrical, the accuracy of the mouth depends on them. What you do with these lines can give the carving a completely different look than one you expected or wanted.*

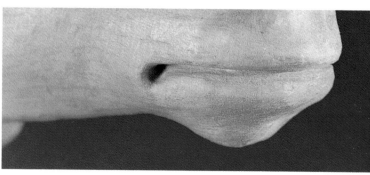

STEP 5) Bring the central lip line to depth, and finish rounding and shaping lips.

Carving the Open Mouth

Observations for the open mouth:
— the position lips take when open.
— the effect of open mouth on nose, cheeks, and eyes.
— the shape, size, and number of teeth and fangs.
— the shape and position of tongue.

STEP 1) Cut the mouth opening in the blank slightly smaller than the extent of the finished opening. *Do this when you blank out on the bandsaw, if possible.*

STEP 2) Shape outside of the mouth as much as possible without actually going inside the mouth. *See Carving the Closed Mouth.*

STEP 3) To get maximum ease, accuracy, and detail inside the mouth, cut the lower jaw off as far back on the neck a possible, but ending the cut just before and inside the corners of the mouth. A very fine jeweler's saw or razor saw is best for this cut.

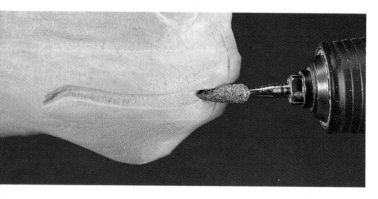

STEP 2) With a narrow flame-shaped ruby carver held in a high angle position, relieve the lip line (the v-shaped groove that is formed where the lips come together). *Inlet the lip line with care and accuracy. Beware! —any deviation up or down could give you a horse with an idiotic grin or a bear that looks down in the dumps.*

STEP 4) Detail the inside of the roof of the mouth, and carve or insert the upper set of teeth. *See Carving Sets of Teeth.*

STEP 5) Detail the inside of the lower jaw. If the tongue is to remain between the teeth, carve it in place or attach it separately, then carve or insert the lower set of teeth. If you want the tongue thrust forward or hanging out over the teeth, finish the teeth first, then carve and fit the tongue to the shape and position desired, and glue it in last.

STEP 6) Reattach lower jaw with epoxy glue. Use a minimum of glue to prevent any from squeezing out into the exposed mouth cavity. Remove any that does with a cotton tip or folded cloth corner before glue sets. *In most cases, finish painting the entire inner mouth before reattaching the jaw will save you hours of frustrating work later.*

STEP 7) Blend jaw back to surrounding areas in preparation for texturing.

Carving Sets of Teeth

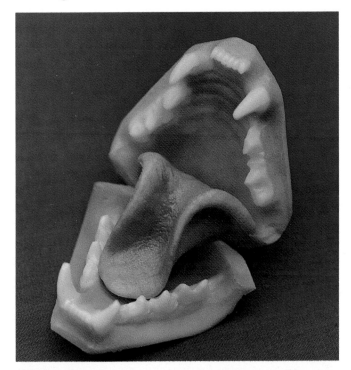

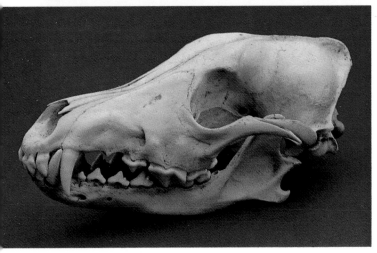

The best reference source for teeth will be a taxidermist or a taxidermist supply house. A few phone calls can generally locate a real skull, or most taxidermy supply houses have a wide variety of animal false teeth sets that are one-time investments for lifetime references.

The method I use most often for making teeth for my carvings is to carve them as one-piece upper and lower sets. The work is picky and time consuming, but the result is well worth the effort.

STEP 1) Draw a line along what would be the gum line just inside the lips. Be as accurate as possible, remembering that the teeth are in a fixed arc and don't necessarily have to follow the lips depending on what the lips are doing.

STEP 2) Relieve the line along the arc with a ball shaped ruby carver. Make sure the resulting groove is a little less in width than the base thickness of the set of teeth that you want to install. The groove should be round bottomed and horseshoe shaped.

STEP 3) Make a paper pattern of the STEP 2 groove by rubbing a soft leaded pencil along the sharp edges of the groove, then laying a small piece of paper over the groove and rubbing the top of the paper with your thumb or the rounded end of a small wooden dowel. The ridges will leave a residue of lead in the shape of the existing groove on the bottom of the paper, allowing you to cut it out and transfer the patterned shape to the piece of stock you will carve the teeth from.

STEP 4) With a bandsaw, jigsaw, or coping saw, cut a horseshoe shaped blank of stock that will fit into the STEP 2 groove. Cut the blank slightly bigger than necessary, and carefully shape the bottom to fit into the groove. *Make sure that the grain of the blank is situated so as to run the length of the teeth and not across them.*

STEP 5) With the blank properly fit in the groove, scribe a line along the top of the groove onto the blank as an indicator for the exposed part of the teeth and the top of the gum line.

STEP 6) Carefully lay out all of the teeth on the stock above the gum line.

STEP 7) Block out the individual teeth. I use a woodburner to deeply outline the individual teeth, then remove whatever stock necessary from between with the tip of a narrow flame-shaped ruby carver.

STEP 8) Finish shape the teeth by carving any curve from front to back, such as the curve found in fangs, then rounding the individual teeth as appropriate with a flame-shaped ruby carver. *Some teeth, such as incisors, will not look as rounded on the sides as molars, which in turn do not look as round as fangs.*

STEP 9) Give the "plate" a final fit by adjusting the bottom as necessary to fit the groove, and glue into place.

STEP 10) Touch up any individual teeth that require it, and blend any irregularities along the glue line.

LEGS, HOOVES, PAWS, & CLAWS

Above all, the feet and legs of a carving have to appear proportionate. If they are carved to perfect detail and texture, they still detract if they are too large or too small. Then, once they are proportionate, they have to be correctly shaped for the task they are performing, whether supporting the animal, involved in some form of action, or at rest.

Its difficult for most of us to recognize how an animal's legs are shaped, because we carve the shape by rote, without recognizing what causes the different shapes underneath the skin. Once you know what causes a particular shape from inside the leg, it's a simple matter to apply the same intellect to practically all species. Why? Because the bones are so similar in most animals, including man, that once we recognize the skeletal structure within a leg we can figure out what causes a particular animal's leg to be shaped the way it is and why. Once we know what bones cause the basic shapes and learn their placement, it becomes a much simpler task to carve them.

Once I came to realize how much I, the human animal, had in common with other animals, the task of learning about them became much easier by comparing their physical and anatomical features to features that I knew about myself. It helps greatly to know that a particular animal has a femur, ulnar, elbow and knee, and how the location causes a particular formation. I found so many commonalities that I began feeling like a cannibal every time I ate meat! *See comparative placement of animal leg bones & joints.*

FRONT/UPPER LIMBS

Reduced to 64%.

1 - *Shoulder*	3 - *Elbow*	5 - *Wrist*	7 - *Metacarpus*
2 - *Humerus*	4 - *Radius/Ulna*	6 - *Carpus*	8 - *Phalanges*

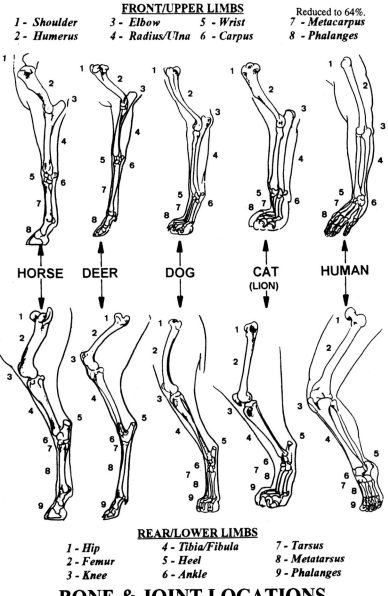

HORSE   DEER   DOG   CAT (LION)   HUMAN

REAR/LOWER LIMBS

1 - *Hip*	4 - *Tibia/Fibula*	7 - *Tarsus*
2 - *Femur*	5 - *Heel*	8 - *Metatarsus*
3 - *Knee*	6 - *Ankle*	9 - *Phalanges*

BONE & JOINT LOCATIONS

Carving hooves, paws, and claws simply requires observation. You can't carve what you don't know or can't visualize. Look at a hoof, not just a quartering view, but from the front, the side, the rear, and the bottom. Note the general outline and shape from every angle, then note details within the general shape.

The little Canadian Lynx that I photographed for references are found in this book gave me one of the greatest opportunities to understand the workings of a cat's paw that I have yet had. Thank heaven he had been declawed, because even in play, I could feel the dexterity and strength in those paws. I let him pull my left hand to his mouth while I held the camera with my right hand, with a fervent prayer that he just wanted a smell. He mouthed my hand, but however gently, I could still feel the remarkable strength of this young cat as he held my hand in place with his paw and jaws. After a playful nip and a couple of licks to my hand, he pulled a little harder and ate my watch, ... almost. Now I know my watch can take a "licking" and keep on ticking! Kodiak, thanks for all you taught me.

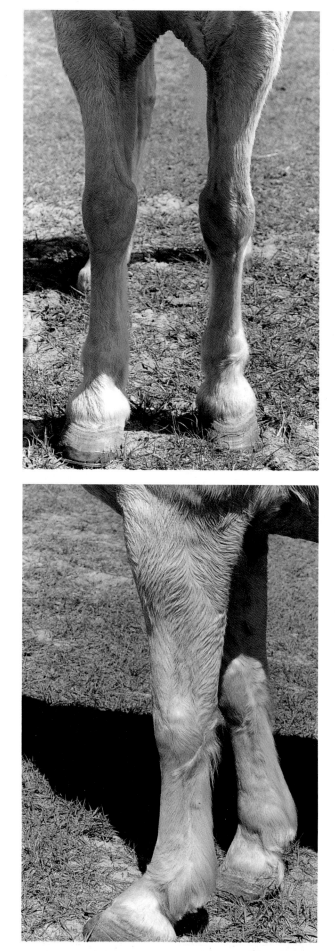

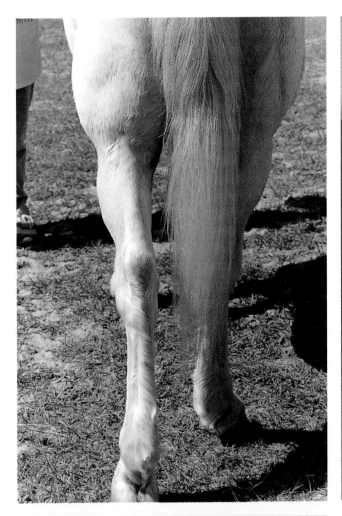

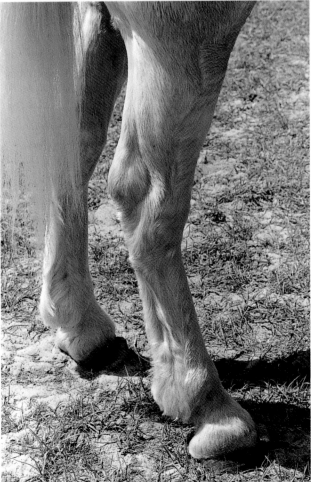

STEP 1) Cut the side-view outlines of the legs as accurately as possible when blanking out.

STEP 2) On the front of the leg, draw a center line in the exact position that you want the leg. *Consider how the leg comes away from the body, how it will give balance to the body, and how it will be positioned with respect to the leg on the other side.*

STEP 3) Draw the correct size and shape of the leg on the blank using the centerline for guidance and symmetry. *All legs should be laid out with pencil at the same time to keep all the legs to scale with respect to one another, and to give proportional prospective to the whole blank.*

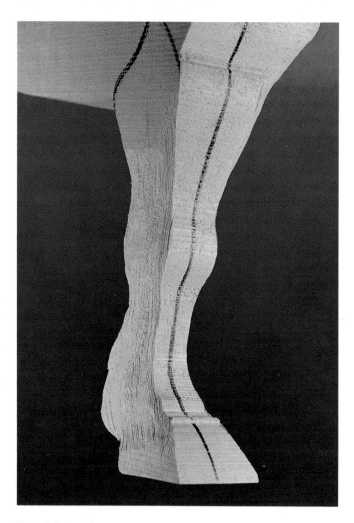

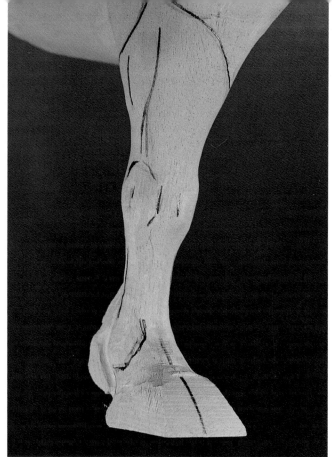

STEP 4) Relieve away the shape of the leg from a front view prospective. The leg should be to size and square shaped at this point.

STEP 5) Round out the leg. *Honor any area that dictates shape such as a joint, ligament depression, the curl/shape of a paw, or the angle of a hoof, by leaving more than enough stock to finish shape the area.*

STEP 6) Locate and layout all of the leg details. Muscle bulges or depressions, extremes and shape of joints, depressions running along the sides of ligaments, creasing or bagging of skin caused by bending or extension, and the extremes of hooves or paws.

STEP 7) Finish shape all details of the legs. *I don't texture fur or hair until the entire carving is complete with every shape and detail exactly as I want it, no matter where the location, so that there is nothing left to do to the carving but to texture fur or hair.*

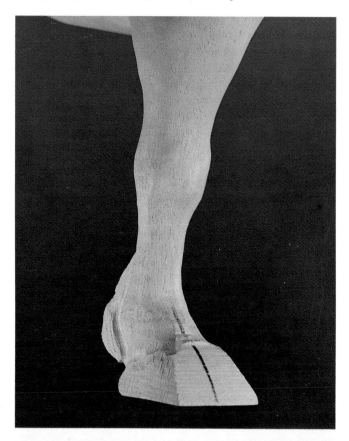

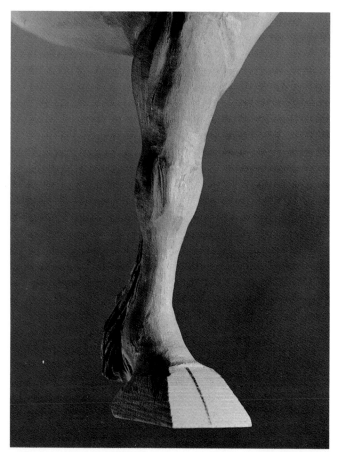

Carving the Paw

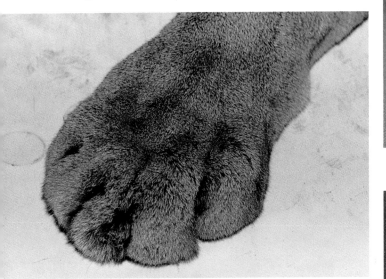

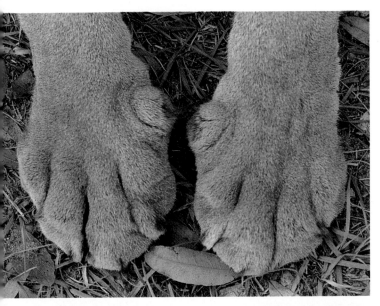

STEP 1) Rough out the paw to approximate the finished position and shape.

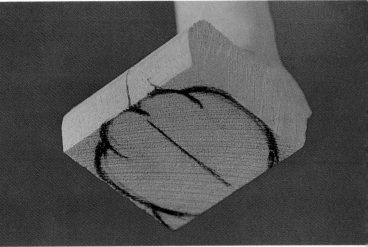

STEP 2) Outline the extremes of the paw on the bottom of the foot.

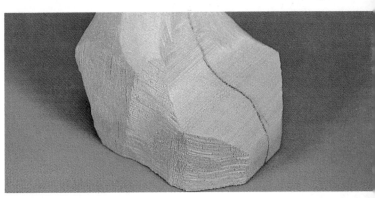

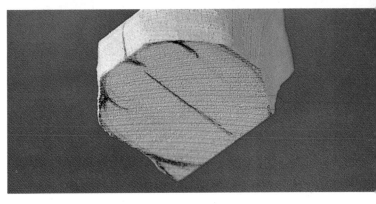

STEP 3) Shape the outline of the paw from the bottom, cutting up and away all the way around the paw.

45

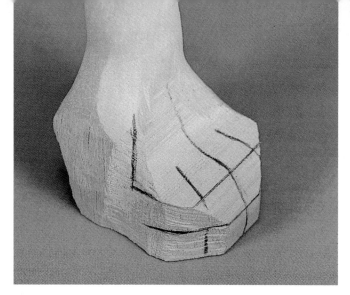

STEP 4) Draw the location of any knuckle ridges around the paw.

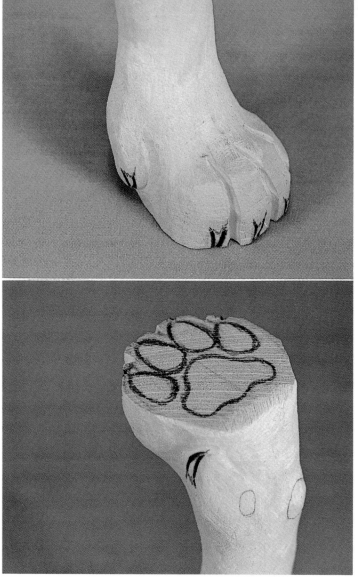

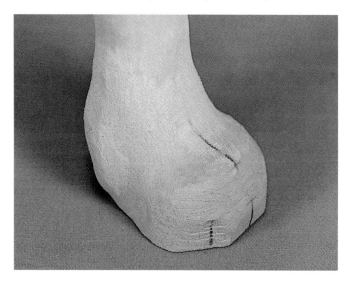

STEP 5) Flatten the surfaces from ridge to ridge, leaving enough stock to relieve away claws from the individual toes that will be dealt with later. Blend the top of the paw into the base of the leg. The paw should now have its finished shape and size with no consideration given to individual toes or claws.

STEP 7) Using a woodburner set at low to medium heat, indent to the extremes of the toe separation, tapering up to nothing where the fur overtakes the exposed separation of the toes. Outline the outer shape of the claws with the woodburner set at a low heat.

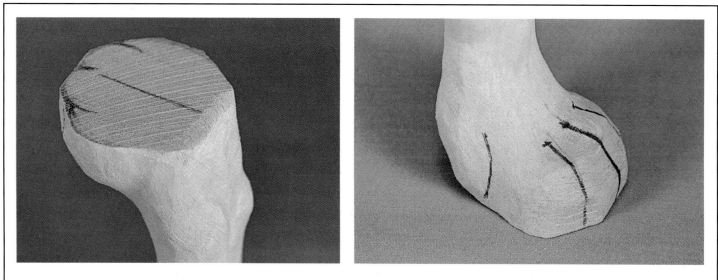

STEP 6) Draw the divisions between the individual toes, and carefully outline the claws at this time.

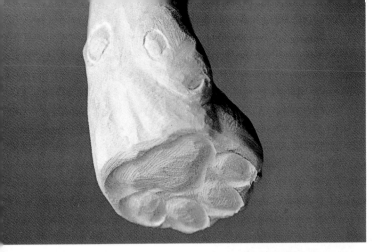

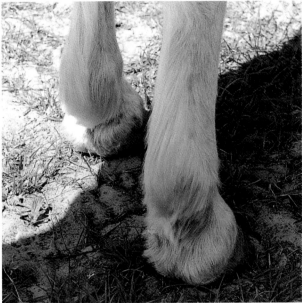

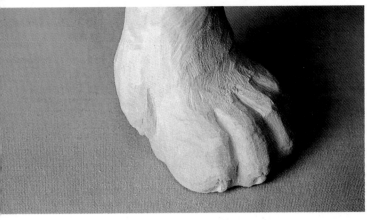

STEP 8) Round out and shape the exposed portion of the individual toes, with the tip of a narrow flame-shaped ruby carver.

STEP 9) Relieve away and shape the claws, using the same bit as in STEP 8. Once the claws are shaped with the ruby carver, I run the side of the woodburner tip set at low heat over the upper exposed portion of the claw in even strokes that blend one into the other, allowing the heat to smooth and set the final shape of the claw. *Use caution and a heat setting just hot enough to brown the wood.*

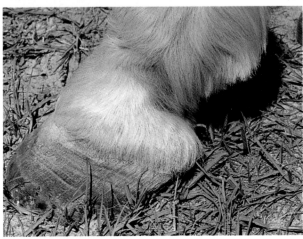

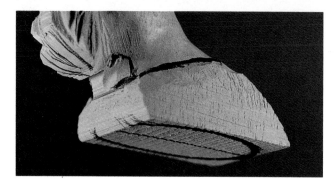

STEP 1) Draw the extremes and all details of the hoof on top and bottom.

STEP 2) Outline the extremes of the hoof on the bottom of the blank.

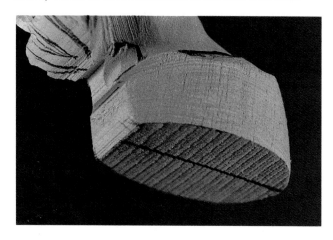

STEP 3) Shape the outline of the hoof from the bottom, cutting up and away all the way around the hoof, using care not to remove necessary stock where the metatarsal joint hangs over the rear of the hoof.

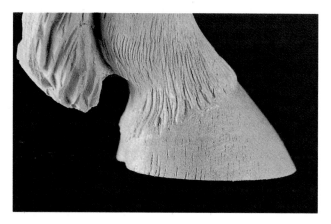

STEP 4) Using the edge of the cut line that outlines the hoof as a guide, round the hoof to shape up to the hair line of the leg, leaving the hoof looking as though it runs under the hair. *Use care, and honor any area where you might want separated strands of hair to hang down over the hoof by leaving enough stock to shape and texture later.*

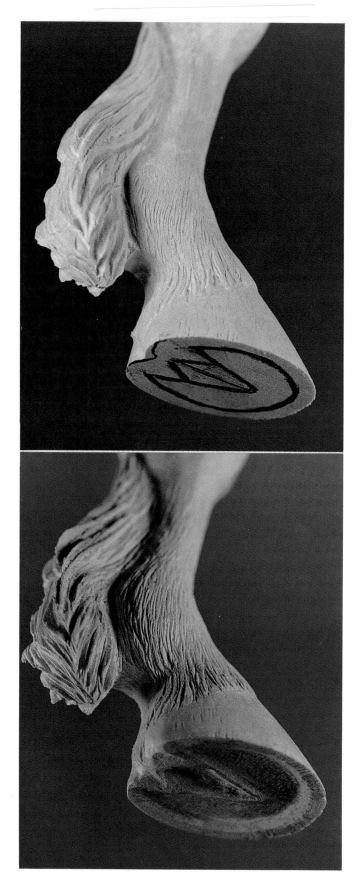

STEP 5) Finish any fine details and blend the hair line back on the leg in preparation for texturing. *If the hoof is lifted, bent up, or in anyway exposed, detail the exposed bottom of the hoof as completely as you did the top.*

48

Hair considerations

Proper scale of the hair to the size of the animal. It's amazing how many carvings are perfectly shaped and posed, and then spoiled by the hair texturing process. Too often the carving is over done by hair that is far too coarse for the size of the animal.

My first deer carving was only about 8" high overall, and I went to great lengths to make sure every area that deserved hair got it — and then some. I finished the carving, and had it displayed at an annual woodcarver's show in Morrisville, Vermont near my home. As I passed time talking with folks, an older man stood looking at that particular carving for some time without saying anything. When the onlookers had thinned somewhat, he said, "I really like that deer, but he must have just come through an extremely hard winter, ... I've hunted them for 45 years and he's about the shaggiest one I've ever seen". I couldn't argue with the truth, and although the texturing was well done, it would have better fit a carving of far greater size. I took a vernier caliper and measured the thickness of hair I put on that carving, and when proportioned against the size of the carving itself, a lifesize carving of that deer would have had to have had individual hairs that were 1" thick!

Size and length of hair on various parts of the body. The differences of coarseness and fineness of hair on the body of a carving go to great lengths in contributing to the three dimensional depth of the carving, especially if the carving is to have a natural finish as opposed to a painted finish. Much can be done to fool the eye through shading and brush strokes with a painted finish, but a natural finish pretty much has to speak for itself.

When I speak of size and length of hair on various parts of the body, I mean the differences between the fine short muzzle hair as compared to the coarse long hair on the back and hump of a grizzly, or the finer back hair on an elk as compared to the shaggy coarse hair on its cape and lower neck. Learn to texture in terms of fine, coarse, soft, and firm **looking** hair. Practice until you can choose the properly shaped stone, grit of stone, and in some case speed of rotation to give you the desired effect you want for a particular texture. Practice on scrap pieces until you get the desired effect and feel the confidence to apply it to your carving.

Effect that the action or pose of the animal has on the hair. The skin pretty much follows the contours caused by the structure of the body. Large muscle masses that join or lie next to smaller muscle masses will cause depressions that the hair covered skin follows. When the animal moves, the muscles flex or stretch with, over, or against other muscle groups, causing some of the hair laying within the major bulge depressions to be jammed into and over hair lying with the depression, giving the area a shaggy coarser look. The action of the animal will determine which areas should be addressed, but attention to detail such as this gives greater depth, detail and appeal to the carving.

Wrinkles of skin caused by action are other areas that require consideration. When the skin wrinkles, the hair at the top of the wrinkle ridges raises and separates, giving a coarser appearance, while the hair at the bottom of the wrinkle ridges compresses, giving a finer, smoother look to the hair.

Carving Hair Separations

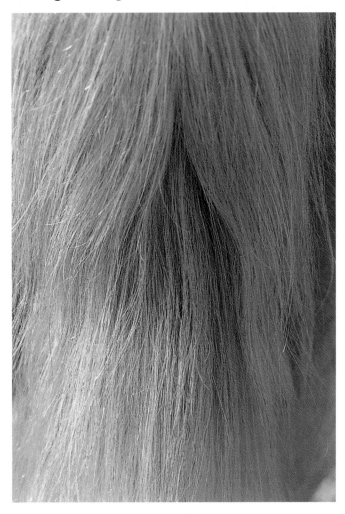

STEP 1) Decide where you want a separation. Separations are formed where upper hair has separated, and hair that would normally lie underneath has pushed through causing the upper hair to remain open or separated. This separation has the schematic shape of an inverted "Y" whose arms and legs all blend back into the mass of hair that they came from. *Separations usually occur with areas of longer hair such as tails and manes, the coarse hump hair on a grizzly bear, the cape hair of a bison, and shaggy longer haired animals. Separations that occur in short haired animals (such as on the side of a horse) are not as obvious, unless the animal is wet — at which time the hair will bunch and separate of its own accord.*

STEP 2) Draw an inverted "Y" to the extent that you want it within the hair mass. Don't overdo the number of separations — a few here and there will be enough to greatly improve the detail and depth of the carving when coupled with texturing.

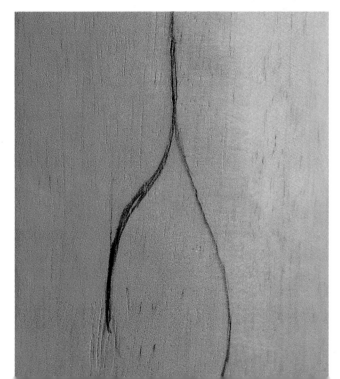

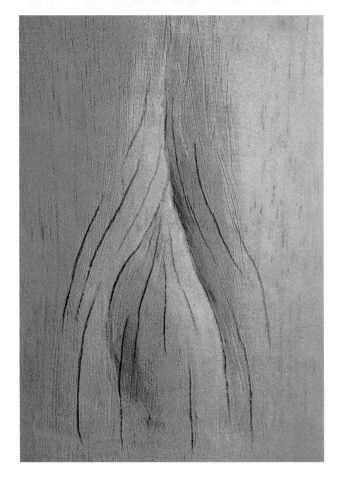

STEP 3) With a narrow flame-shaped ruby carver, draw your stroke along the legs of the "Y" with the greatest depth at the crotch of the "Y", and shallowing out to match the surface at the tips of the legs.

STEP 5) Texture during final texturing operation.

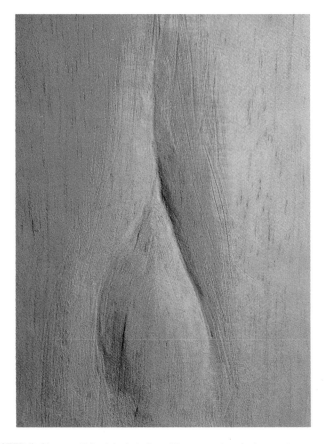

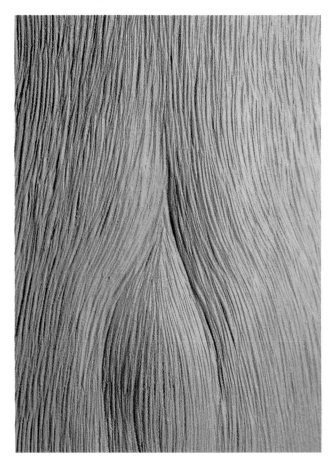

STEP 4) Shape and blend the hair that will appear to be spewing out from the separated hair above it. Slightly roll the shape of the separated upper hair and blend outer edges back into the hair mass.

Step 6 Accent desired areas with a woodburner at low heat.

50

Carving Hair Overlays

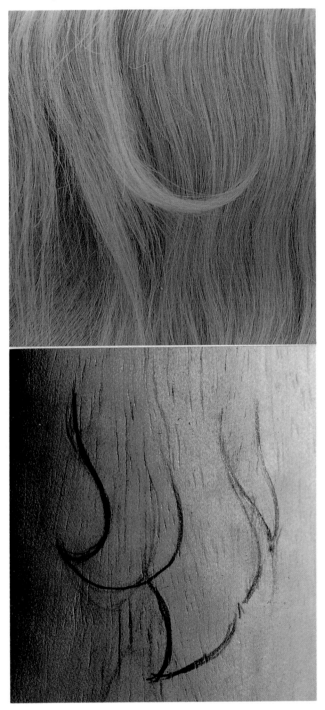

STEP 2) Using a flame-shaped ruby carver, relieve the upper hair away from the lower hair by outlining the shape of the upper hair mass. Define the sides of the upper hair by matching the depth of the lower or bottom cut and allowing the cut to shallow out as it blends upwards into the existing surface.

STEP 1) Decide where you want a hair overlay and draw the extent of it in place. Hair overlays can be caused by a few hairs or bunches of hair separating away and coming back to lay over the hair below it, out of place and usually in a different direction. The primary detail on an overlay is the ledge formed by the hair above as it lays over the hair below. *Overlays occur most often in areas of shaggy hair such as capes, manes, tails, and the coats of long haired animals.*

STEP 3) Remove stock from around sides and bottom of upper hair shape.

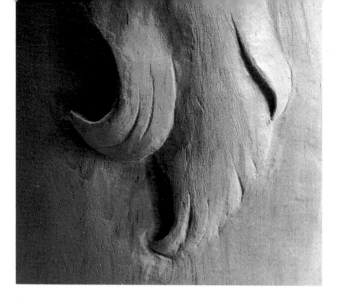

STEP 4) Finish shape upper hair mass. Shape and undercut the area of any curl(s) to give greater depth and detail to the carving. Blend upper extremes as necessary.

STEP 5) Lay out flow lines and texture during final texturing operation.

Texturing Hair

STEP 1) Make sure that the entire body is finish shaped and smoothed. Texturing should be one of the last carving operations. The tail, and animals with manes should have the tail/mane shapes completely formed and ready to texture. Any curled hair, separations, and hair overlay areas should be finish shaped. *See Carving Hair Separations and Overlays.*

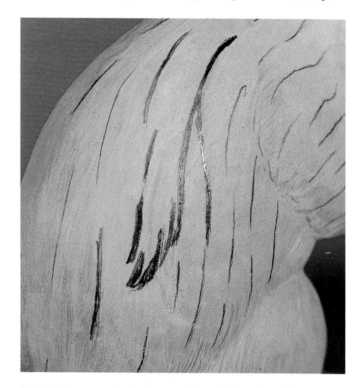

STEP 2) From your animal references, give careful attention to the manner in which the hair is patterned or flows on the animal. Once you perceive the "lay of the hair", lightly draw flow lines over the entire body. *Flow lines are penciled lines that indicate the direction the hair takes on the body — the direction it takes off the back and down the sides, along the stomach, away from the nose, off the muzzle, off the forehead, along the neck, etc.*

STEP 3) Within the flow lines, look for areas that would be appropriate for hair separations or hair overlays, and draw them in with heavier darker lines. *See Carving Hair Separations and Overlays.*

STEP 4) Hold the carving at arm's length and look it over. If there are lines that don't seem to follow the flow or blend gracefully enough to suit you, erase and redraw them, because these are the guides by which you will texture.

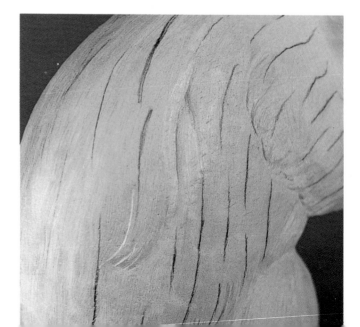

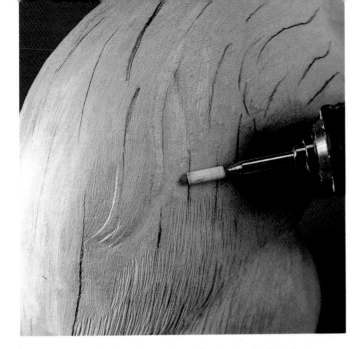

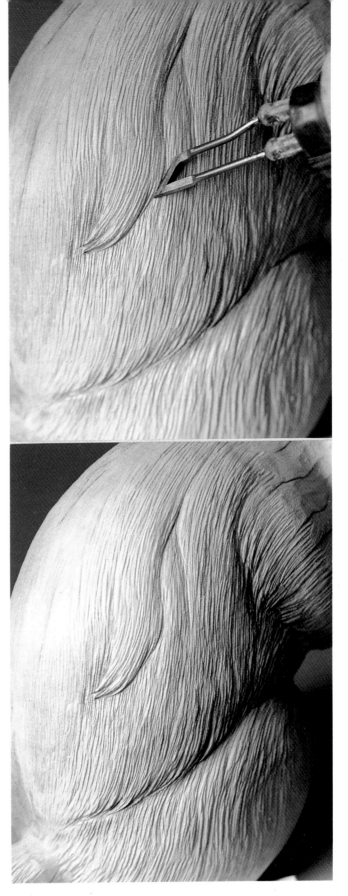

STEP 5) With a cylinder or inverted cone shaped stone, begin texturing the carving **from the bottom working upwards,** and from the rear working forward wherever possible. Use the very edge of the stone held in a high angle so that the edge cuts a tiny "V" groove. Work from side to side, using zigzag strokes in uneven rows. Overlapping the row already finished, do the same thing over again, with occasional longer strokes running through the row below. *The longer strokes through the row below will not only tie the overlapping rows together, but will lend a better look of direction to the overall mass. If you find an area where you feel a bit of additional detail is needed, make a deeper cut by applying a bit more pressure to your stroke. This will give the appearance of a straight hair separation. Remember to keep the deeper cut in the same direction as the texture lines that surround it, and texture the sides of the cut so that all the hairs appear to be the same scale.*

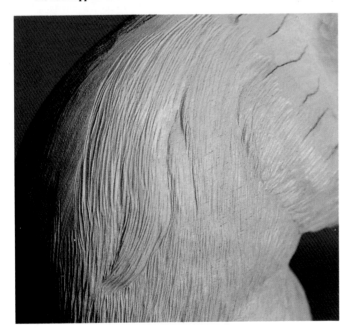

STEP 6) In areas where you have occasion to work against end grains, the wood will sometimes lift, causing "fuzzing" to occur (especially with a wood like basswood). The fuzz can be removed or made to lie down by use of a rotary bristle brush at slow speed working with the grain. The brush is also a good way to totally clean the areas already textured in preparation for sealing and painting. Work with the direction of the texture when cleaning, and not across it, as the brush may remove some of the detail if too much pressure is used. *Prepare a new rotary bristle brush for use by crumbling it in between the fingers. This spreads the individual bristles and "softens" the brush for use.*

STEP 7) Finally, if the carving is to be painted, small areas where greater depth between individual hairs or groups is desired, can be accented with a woodburner. I use a skew shaped woodburning tip at medium heat, held at a high angle, and pull my strokes, lifting away towards the burner tip to feather the indentation. Always place these accent marks in the direction of the existing textured hair or fur.

When carving an animal with antlers, one of the main considerations to the completion of that animal, is the best method to use to achieve an accurate and detailed rack; however, above all else a rack with the strength to withstand occasional handling, movement from place to place, and the stress and aging imposed by ownership (both present and posterity). It saddens me to see a beautiful piece that has been broken because of poor grain placement or incompetent construction.

I attended a woodcarvers banquet where a lovely little child won a carving of a carousel horse in one of the prize drawings. The child was thrilled, and as a child, chose to play with the carving immediately by pushing all the tableware away and clearing a little "pasture" for her pony. The minute she set the horse down, two of the legs broke off. Inspection revealed that whoever carved the horse had carved it with the grain running across the legs instead of up them for strength. Before the evening was over, one other leg broke, and one of the broken legs broke again.

Although the horse's legs have nothing to do with antlers, the same consideration for strength that should have been used for the horse's legs has to be used when selecting the method by which antlers will be carved or formed.

The three primary methods I use are:

<u>Method One</u> — carving the antler set completely from wood — this method is most commonly used when the carving is to be of a natural or wood grain finish and no foreign material is desired to interrupt or detract from the beauty of the wood grain.

When I carve antlers from wood alone, I arrange the antler pattern on the wood in a manner that the grain will run as closely in the direction of the antler mass as I can arrange it. I gain maximum strength by running with the grain, doing my best to locate within the grain for a minimum of weak or cross-grain spots. I have used burly wood where the grain runs in all directions with good success for this type of antler. It also make a beautiful grain for bodies.

<u>Method Two</u> — carving the antler set from wood, but strength within the antlers is achieved by lamination or doweling within the cross-grained areas that present weaknesses. This method is perfectly acceptable when the antlers are to be painted or stained and shadowed. Laminating the wood in a way which causes the grain to run along the beams and tines is quite simple.

Pinning the tines — if possible, I pin the points as far along their lengths as I can by drilling up through the cross-grained areas, pinning with brass wire, and gluing with 5 minute epoxy glue. I fill the tiny holes with a glue/dust mixture made from the same piece of wood as was used to cut the antlers.

<u>Method Three</u> — fabrication of the antler set with a material other than wood, usually metal with epoxy paste as fill and model medium. Since I paint the majority of my antlered animals, this is the method I use most of the time. The materials used are combinations of brass welding rods, solid copper wires, silver solder, and epoxy paste. The size of the rack I'm making determines the gauge of the wire and the diameter of the brass welding rod.

Although antler sets can be cast very nicely in pewter, or with an epoxy resin/powdered additive mixture, it is very time consuming, and requires specific tools and materials. This is quite costly unless the same set of antlers is to be cast and recast for use with production carvings.

Antler terminology

Horn — a permanent bone-like appendage usually terminating in a point.
Antler — a calcified appendage shed or dropped annually.
Tine — any tapered spike terminating in a point, standing up (sometimes down and sideways) from a beam. Tines are often referred to as points.
Tine Base — the bottom portion of the tine where it spreads and blends into the beam.
Beam or Main Beam — the heavier mass of antler that emerges directly from the animal's head, supports all the points, and terminates in a tapering point.
Beam Base — the knurled and knotty portion of the beam where it attaches to the head.
Branch — one side or the other of the rack, or a division of the beam on one side.
Rack — the entire structure of beams and points comprising of the antlers.
Fork — the spreading of two points or the place where the beam and point(s) form a crotch or "V"
Spread — the widest side-to-side dimension between the main beams.
Brow Tines or Points — the first two points emerging from the beam bases on either side — so named for their proximity to the brows of the eyes.
Palmate — the mass of webbing between beam and tines, or between tines. Called palmation because it resembles the palm of a hand with the fingers spread. *Moose and caribou have areas of palmation on their antlers.*

Making Metal Antler Sets

The size of the animal determines what gauge solid copper wire or brass rod I use to make the antler set. The brass brazing rod comes in a variety of sizes and can be purchased from any welding supply business. The solid copper wire can be purchased from building supply firms in sizes up to 1/4" or more depending on the supplier.

Use caution during the construction of antlers. I have had more mishaps while making metal antlers than during any other process connected with carving. My greatest concern is for my eyes, and to date nothing adverse has happened, because I always wear heavy duty goggles. However, during the initial learning process, I suffered several minor finger burns, scratches, and cuts to my fingers. Now I use clamps, gloves, solder aids and anything else that will keep me from pain, with the most effective aid being common sense.

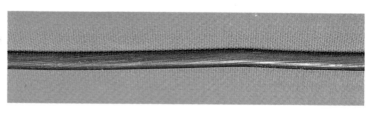

STEP 1) Cut beams to a length that will accommodate the number of tines desired, with additional stock left at the beam bases for anchoring into pre-drilled and shaped head holes.

STEP 2) Bend tine stock to 90 degree angle.

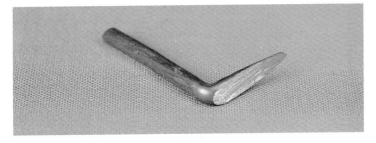

STEP 3) Cut vertical leg to desired length of tine.

STEP 4) Cut horizontal leg to a length suitable for soldering to beam, and grind or file the bottom to a flat tapering wedge.

STEP 5) Grind or file a flat surface the size of the tine soldering tang on the beam, located so as to nearly match a mate across from it on the other beam.

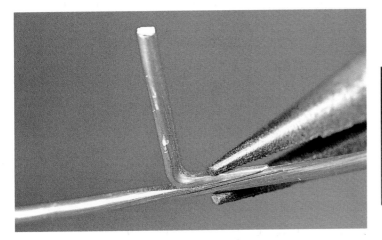

STEP 6) Coat tine & beam flats with soldering flux, clamp in position, and solder with soft to medium silver solder using a suitable torch. *A solder clamp with a heat sink or steel needle-nosed pliers with a heavy rubber band around the handles for pressure have worked for me for years. BEWARE! When using tongs, douse the work in water before touching it with your fingers!*

STEP 7) Position and solder all tines on both branches before going further.

STEP 8) Taper and point the tines and the beam tips by grinding or rotary sanding. I grind the metal to shape with a pear shaped serrated carbide bit with **just enough speed** to remove stock. *Keep your holding hand clear of the antlers by clamping them in a hand-held jeweler's vise or vise grips.*

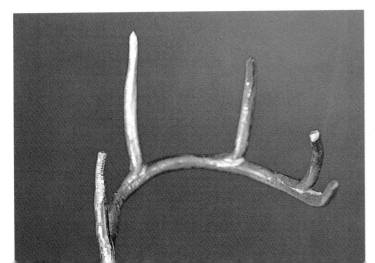

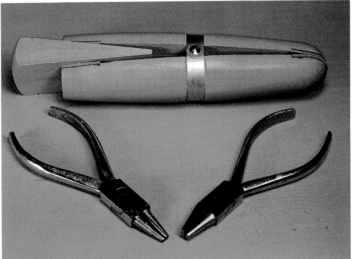

STEP 9) Bend beams to desired shape. When both beam branches are in place, they should describe an oval. Continuously position the antlers in the head anchoring holes during the bending process until the desired shape, spread, and angle is achieved. *Use two pairs of round-jawed jeweler's pliers to make the bends, as square-edged jaws will mar the beams or tines as they are being bent. If a squared bend is needed, then pliers and/ or a clamp with squared jaws are used.*

STEP 10) Bend all tines to final position and shape. *Tines should not be bent again after epoxy paste is in place.*

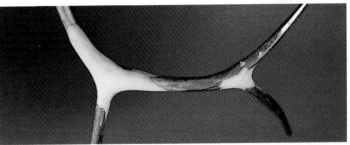

STEP 11) Mix and place epoxy paste to fill and finish shape tine bases, to build beam bases to tapered thickness, and to fill any irregularities at solder joints.

STEP 12) Sand or file hardened paste areas to shape. Give special attention to shaping and blending the tine bases back to the beams, and the thickness of the base as it terminates at the irregular ring where the antler meets the skull.

STEP 13) Relieve away the irregular bumps and grooves running down the bases of the beams, and sand or grind any other desired textures in the antlers. Inspect antlers thoroughly for any rough or unfinished areas.

STEP 14) Cover antlers (except anchor tabs) entirely with two or three coats of lacquer as a base to accept paint. If acrylic paints are to be used for finish, use an acrylic lacquer; if oil base paints, use appropriate lacquer.

STEP 15) The easiest way to cover and color the antlers is to use an air brush or spray can to apply the base color, shade and blend additional colors by the same method, then wash the entire rack with a brush and antiquing liquid to accentuate any textures and depressions.

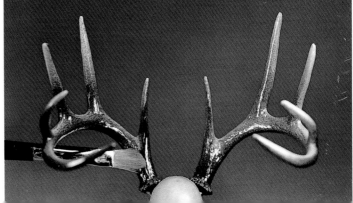

V PROJECT PLANS

Black Bear

Rear

GRAIN

Front

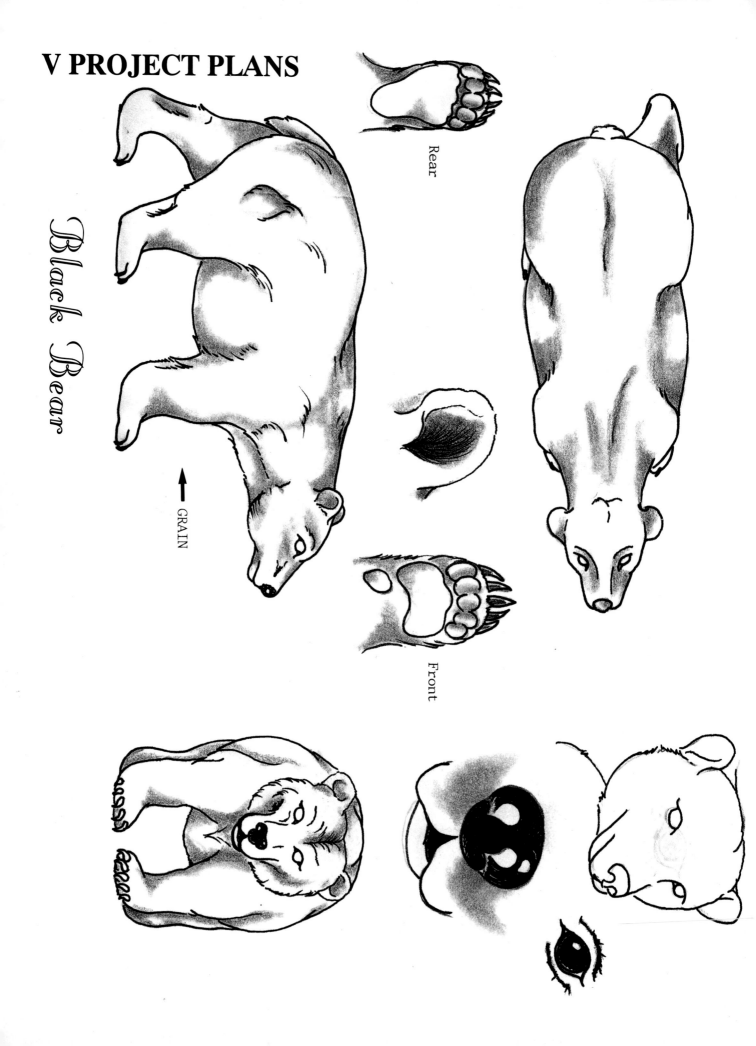

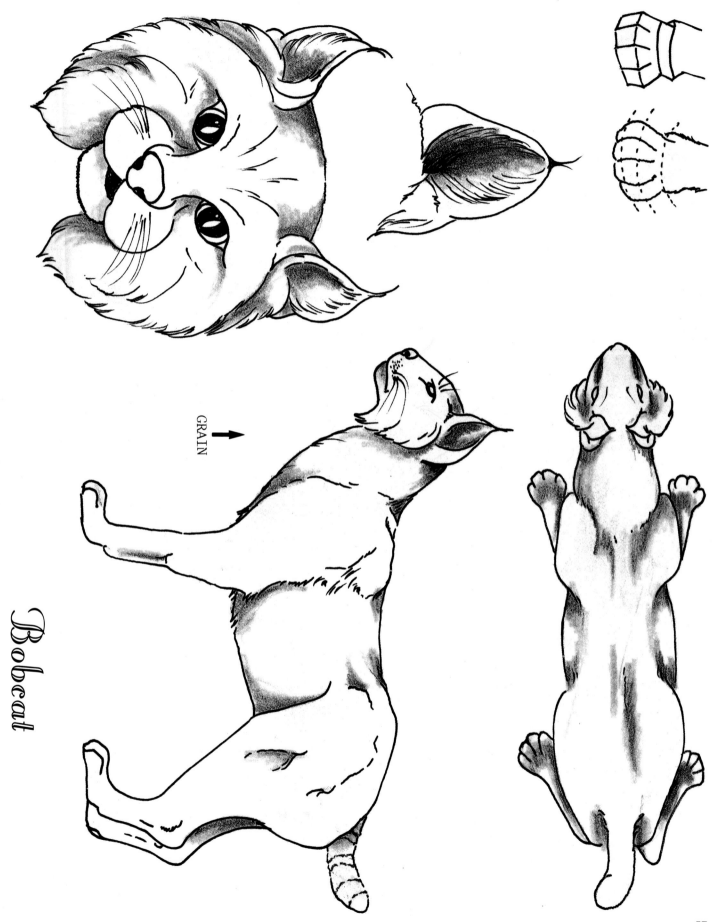

GRAIN →

Bobcat

Bison

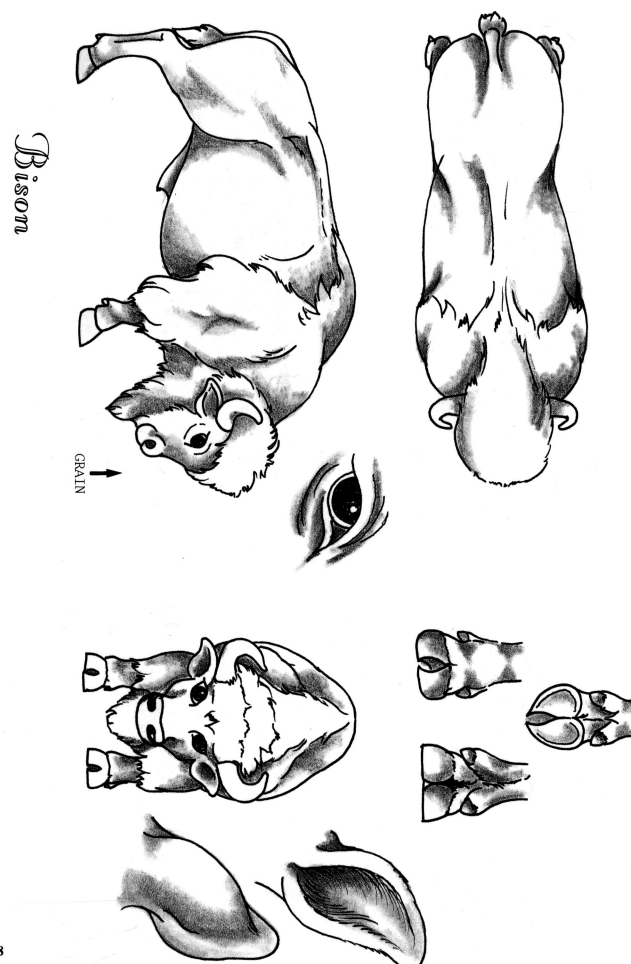

GRAIN

58

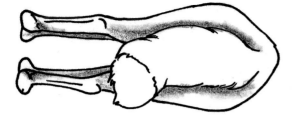

Fox

GRAIN

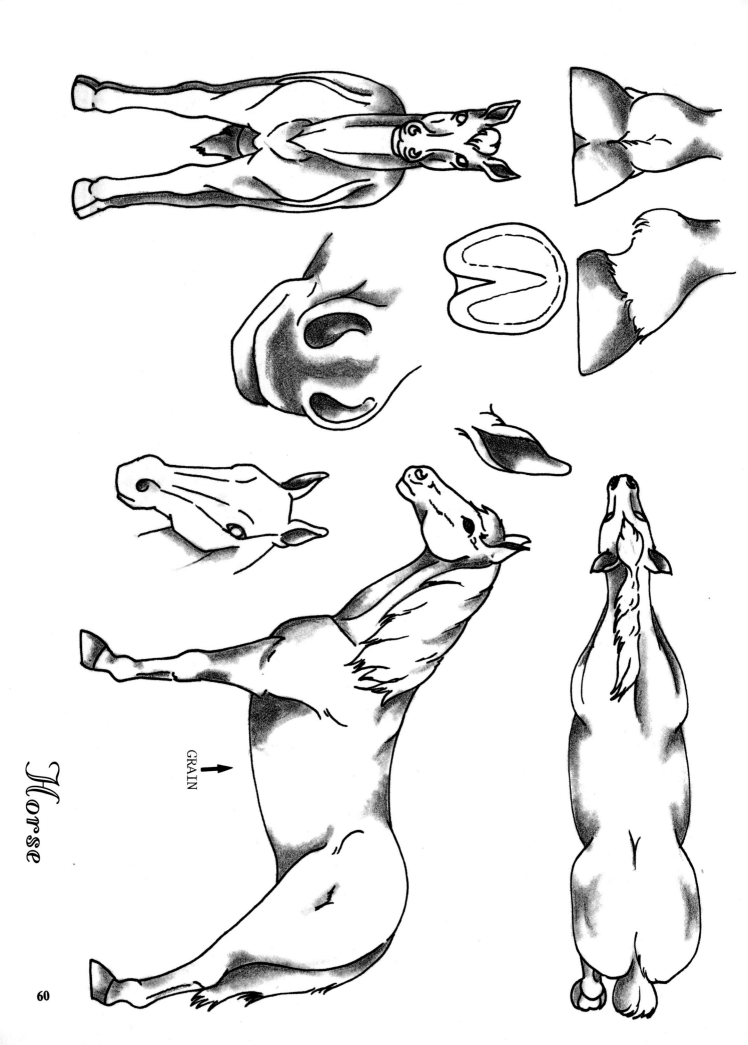

Horse

GRAIN

60

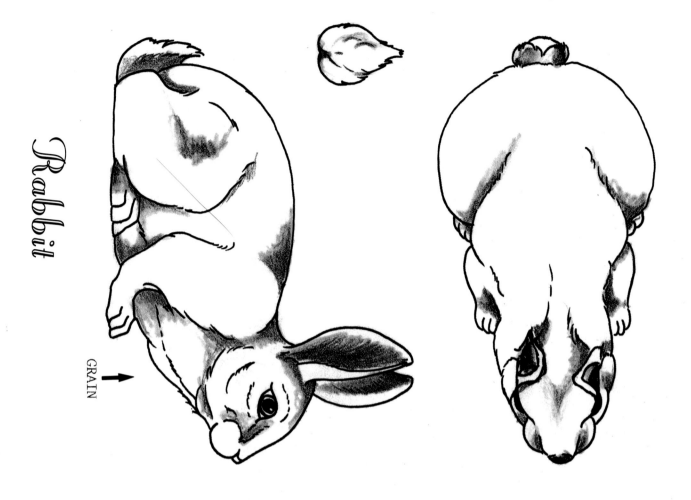

Rabbit

GRAIN

Front

Rear

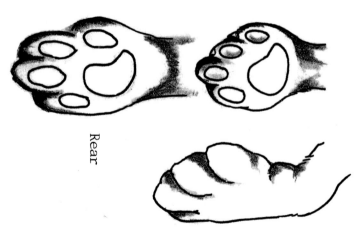

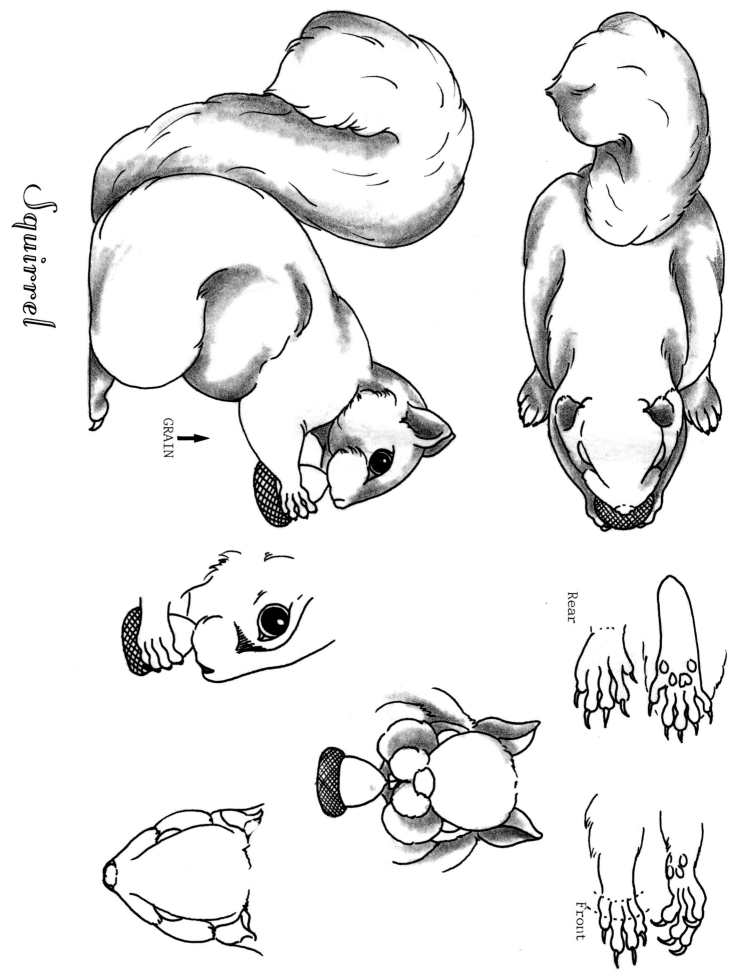

Squirrel

GRAIN

Rear

Front

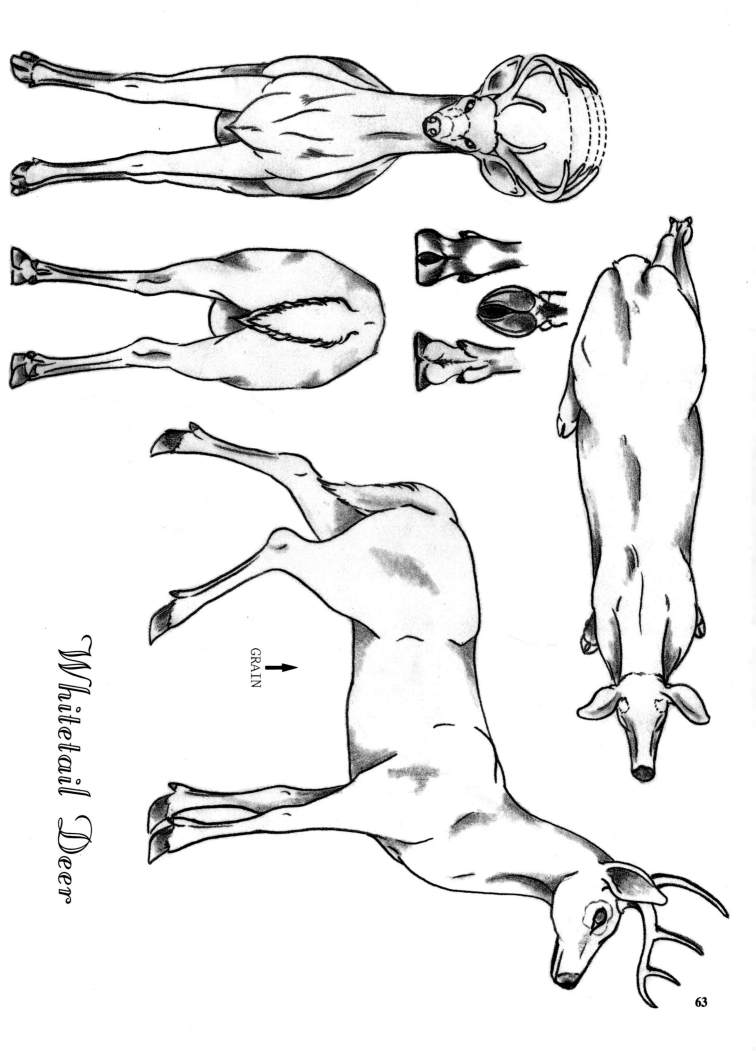

Whitetail Deer

GRAIN

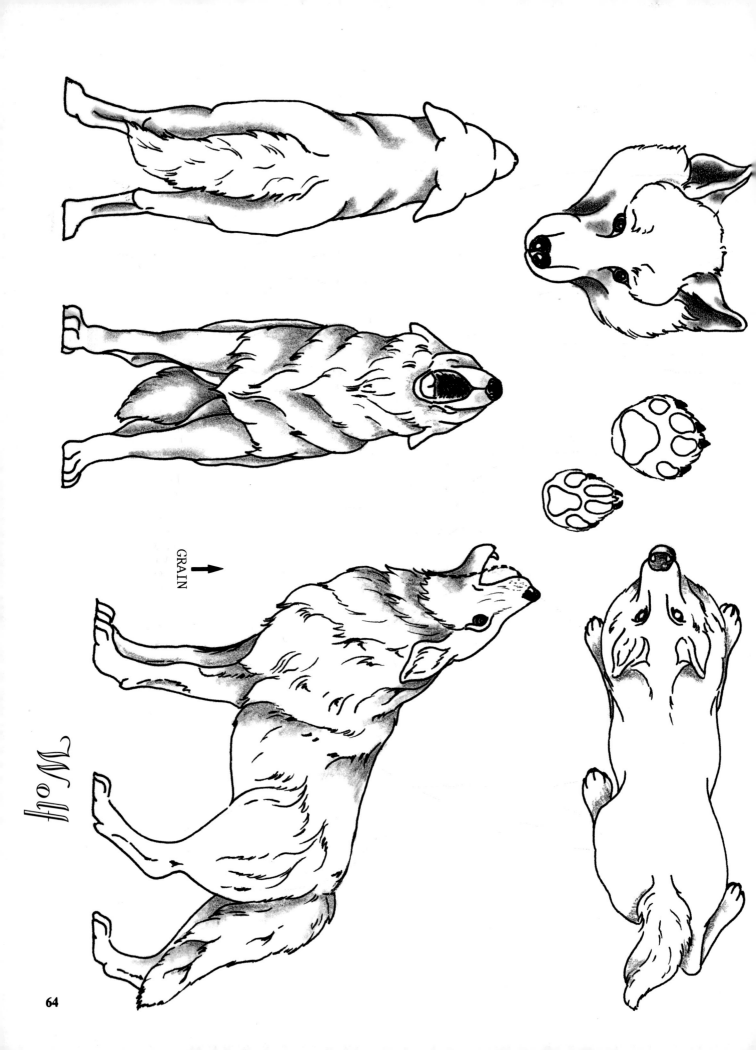

GRAIN →

Wolf